200 Celebrities Who Changed Their Names and How They Found Success

I0140609

© 2015 by Stanley J. St. Clair,
St. Clair Publications

ISBN 978-1-935786-90-0

Printed in the United States of America

St. Clair Publications
P. O. Box 726
Mc Minnville, TN 37111-0726

http://stclairpublications.com

Cover Design by Kent Hesselbein
© 2015 KGH Design Studio

http://www.kghdesignstudio.com/services.html

200 Celebrities Who Changed Their Names

And How They Found Success

Stanley J. St. Clair

Best-selling Author of
*Most Comprehensive Origins of Clichés,
Proverbs and Figurative Expressions*

INTRODUCTION

There are numerous reasons why persons in the public eye change their names (or have it done for them). Many times it is simply because their birth names are too long, complex, ethnic, or would be difficult to pronounce or remember. Some have taken their mother's maiden names, or the surname of a stepfather or first husband which was never dropped. But many others are much more complex. For instance, why did Rudolf Walter Wanderone, Jr. and James A. Moore, Jr. both take the names of fictional characters that they claimed were based on them and how did doing so change their lives forever?

At least 20 featured entertainers who took stage names were from Jewish immigrant families. Many were impoverished; some were abused; several were forced to work as young children to help pay family bills. Many were from broken homes, and some never knew their biological fathers, often being placed in foster care. One worked as a prostitute, one a bootlegger; another was a drug dealer. Several were jailed. One was expelled from school and many were dropouts. How did these broken individuals climb to the top of their professions? It took dogged determination and encouragement, and likely, a new name.

In this pictorial book of trivia, one unique feature is that I include popular actors, singers, dancers, authors, sports figures, magicians, entrepreneurs, broadcasters, models and others who longed to create a public persona which he or she felt was worthy of his or her audience, revealing the circumstances and reasons behind the changes and how they built the public perceptions which took them up the ladder of success. I have been very selective in order to provide a variety of intriguing personalities and stories of overcoming adversity.

**Actress Ann Harding and Second Husband,
Famed Classical Conductor and Composer,
Werner Janssen
(Photo Compliments of Barbara Badger Janssen,
Werner's Granddaughter)**

Nick Adams (July 10, 1931 – February 7, 1968) American film and television actor and screenwriter

Birth Name — Nicholas Aloysius Adamschock

1959 ABC TV Photo, Public Domain Born in Nanticoke, Pennsylvania, Nick's father was a Ukrainian-born coal miner. In 1958 he related how the family lived in a little company house and was always in debt to the company store. The family left at his age five when his uncle was killed in a mining accident. When the car ran out of gas in New Jersey, Nick's dad was given work as a janitor. In high school Adams turned down a job as a minor league baseball player, and briefly worked as a bat boy for the Jersey City Giants.

While visiting New York, Nick wandered into a play audition and met **Jack Palance**, whose father was also a Ukrainian coal miner. When he asked Adams why he wanted to act, he said, "For the money." Palance then introduced him to the director of the play as Nick Adams.[1] Though he didn't get hired, Palance sent him to a junior theater group where he got his first acting job playing Muff Potter in *Tom Sawyer*. The name stuck. He is best remembered as Johnny Yuma, *The Rebel* on ABC (1959).

Alan Alda (January 28, 1936-_____) American actor, director, screenwriter and author
Birth Name — Alphonso d'Abruzzo

1960's Photo, *Friedman-Abeles*, NY,
Public Domain

Alda was born in New York City and traveled around the country with his father's work in burlesque. In spite of physical and situational setbacks during childhood, Alda became an icon of television, primarily due to his first major role as Hawkeye Pierce on *M*A*S*H*, which stretched the short Korean War out to over 10 years from September 17, 1972 – February 28, 1983.

Wanting to shorten his complex name, this six-time Emmy winner concocted the new surname by combining the first two letters of his first and last names.[2] His father, Robert, and his brother Antony also took the name Alda.

He has also had numerous other roles during the years following *M*A*S*H*, which Alda felt made a political statement.

Woody Allen (December 1, 1935-_____) American actor, writer, director, playwright, comedian and musician
Birth Name — Allen Konigsberg

1970s Photo by *Jerry Kupcinet*,
Creative Commons Attribution- Share Alike, OTRS

Born in the Bronx and raised in Brooklyn, New York, Allen was the son of a jewelry engraver father and a mother who kept books for her family's delicatessen. His Ashkenazi Jewish grandparents immigrated from Russia and Austria, and spoke Yiddish, Hebrew, and German. At the age of 17, this to-be-famed director-actor-comedian changed his name to Heywood Allen. Later he shortened it to "Woody" Allen.[3] Before becoming an actor, Allen worked as a comedy writer for TV, also writing short, humorous books. Then in the 1960s, he began doing standup comedy using monologues. In these he developed a persona as being nerdish and insecure. But this is a far cry from the real Allen. He was ranked fourth as all-time greatest standup comedians of all time by *Comedy Central* in 2004. In addition to this, his 24 Academy Award nominated screenplays have made him a great force in Hollywood. He also plays regularly as a jazz clarinetist in small Manhattan clubs.

9

Julie Andrews (October 1, 1935-_____) English film and stage actress, singer, author, theatre director and dancer
Birth Name — Julia Elizabeth Wells

1965 Fox Publicity Photo, Public Domain

"Julie" was born in Walton-on-the-Thames, Surry, England. Conceived as the result of an affair, Andrews was misled about the identity of her biological father. When she found out the truth at age 15, she changed her name to match his.[4]

Andrews had started performing on stage by age 10, and her American Broadway debut was on September 30, 1954, on the eve of her 19th birthday. Her film debut was ten years later in *Mary Poppins*, for which she won an Oscar for Best Actress, followed by another nomination the following year for *The Sound of Music*. She went on to star in many more memorable roles.

Andrews has recently written children's books.

Marc Anthony (September 16, 1968-_____) American actor, singer, and record and television producer
Birth Name — Marco Antonio Muñiz

Disney Wikia Photo – Fair use

Anthony was born in New York City to parents from Puerto Rico. This well-known figure is a lot more than just JLo's ex. He is a 2-time Grammy and 5-time Latin Grammy winning singer who has sold more than 12,000,000 albums worldwide. He has also won numerous other awards and honors, including the 2009 *Congressional Hispanic Caucus Institute Chair's Lifetime Achievement Award*, and he's just in his prime. And he acts and has produced records and television shows with **Simon Fuller**.

Anthony grew up in East Harlem. His name has never been legally changed. His Puerto Rican parents named him after the popular Mexican singer by the same name. He felt that could not use his birth name so he changed it for recording to avoid confusion.[5]

11

Desi Arnaz (March 2, 1917- December 2, 1986) Cuban-born American musician, comedian, actor and television producer
Birth Name — Desiderio Albert Arnaz y De Acha III

1950s Photo, Gen. Artists Corp. (PD)

Born in Santiago do Cuba, unlike many future stars, Arnaz was not from a traditionally poor family. His father was the youngest ever mayor of his Cuban town and served in the Cuban House of Representatives. According to Desi's 1976 autobiography, the family once owned three ranches, a palatial home and a vacation mansion on a private island. Following the Cuban Revolution in 1933, his father was arrested and jailed, and all property confiscated. After his release, the family moved to Miami.

Following his schooling, Desi turned to show business, landing a Broadway starring role in *Too Many Girls* in 1939. He went to Hollywood the next year to resume the role in the film version starring **Lucille Ball**. They were married November 30, 1940, and a great career was launched resulting in their popular TV show, *I Love Lucy* in 1951. His name was officially shortened during his stint in the army in WW II.[6]

Bea Arthur (May 13, 1922 – April 25, 2009) American actress, comedian and singer
Birth Name — Bernice Frankel

1973 CBS Publicity Photo, Public Domain

Born in New York City, the family moved to Cambridge, Maryland at her age 11. When she enlisted in the Marines in 1941, at age 21, she used the name Bernice Frankel. She briefly married Private Robert Arthur. She took his name and never changed it again.[7]

With a career spanning seven decades, this television icon was made famous to her TV fans by her Emmy-Winning role as Maude Finley in *All in the Family* and *Maude* and immortal as Dorothy Zbornak on the *Golden Girls,* for which she also garnered an Emmy. Many do not realize, however, that she had won a Tony (Best Featured Actress in a Musical) even earlier for her portrayal of Vera Charles in the original cast of *Mame* in 1966, and had been a member of an Off-Broadway theater company since the late 1940s, and On Broadway since 1966 in *Fiddler on the Roof.* She had also been a regular on **Sid Caesar**'s TV show in 1954. She was Jewish, an outspoken liberal Democrat, and a lifelong supporter of animal rights.

Fred Astaire (May 10, 1899 – June 22, 1987) American Dancer, singer, musician and actor

Birth Name -- Frederick Austerlitz

1943 Publicity Photo, Public Domain

Born in Omaha, Nebraska to a Jewish immigrant father turned Catholic and a German Lutheran mother, his mother suggested changing their family name to Astaire,[8] saying that Austerlitz sounded like the name of a battle. He had one sister, Adele, who showed great talent in dancing and singing as a child. After his father lost his job, the family moved to New York in 1905 where their mother planned to prepare their children for jobs in show business. He and his sister, Adele, were taught dance, speaking and singing. Their first act was dubbed, *Juvenile Artists Presenting an Electric Musical Toe-Dancing Novelty.* A local paper wrote that they were the greatest child act in vaudeville. Fred went on to appear on Broadway, then in films and television. His career as a dancer and actor spanned 76 years. He was best known for his dancing partnership and on and off screen romantic interest in **Ginger Rogers**. He was named the fifth *Greatest Male Star of All Time* by the American Film Institute.

14

Charles Atlas (October 30, 1892 – December 24, 1972) Italian-born
American bodybuilding method developer and strongman
Birth Name — Angelo Siciliano

1920s Ad, Public Domain

Born in Acri, Calabria, Italy, Angelo moved with his family to Brooklyn,
New York at his age 11. According to his later ads, as a youth he was a
"97 pound weakling." One day at the beech a bully kicked sand in his
face. Desiring to improve his physique, he tried weight lifting and other
methods. Inspired by strongmen such as **Eugen Sando** and **Bernarr
McFadden**, and too poor to join the YMCA, he read *Physical Culture*
magazine, attended strongman shows on Coney Island then questioned
the strongmen afterward. Finally he developed his own system of
exercises called *Dynamic Tension*, a phrase coined by Charles Roman. In
1921 McFadden, publisher of *Physical Culture*, called him America's most
handsome man. In 1922, at age 30, he officially changed his name to
Charles Atlas. The name Charles likely came from Charles Roman who
worked with him to develop his system. Atlas was because a friend told
him he resembled the statue of Atlas on top of a hotel in Coney Island.[9]
Placing ads in comic books and magazines, he sold courses by mail order
and became the most popular muscleman of his day.

15

Gene Autry (September 29, 1907 – October 2, 1998) American singing cowboy hero and actor
Birth Name – Orvon Grover Autry

1940's Publicity Photo, Public Domain

Born in Toiga, Texas, his family moved to southern Oklahoma in the 1920s. After high school Autry worked as a telegrapher, and would sing and play his guitar to pass the lonely hours. One night he was heard by famed humorist, **Will Rogers**, who told him to sing professionally. He went to New York and auditioned for RCA Victor. He was told to go get some experience on the radio and come back. He got on Tulsa's WVOO as Oklahoma's Yodeling Cowboy. The next year he was signed by Capitol Records. Autry was made immortal for his clean-cut image, 93 films, 91 television shows and Western classic records like *Back in the Saddle Again, Silver Haired Daddy of Mine,* and Christmas standards like *Here Comes Santa Clause* and *Rudolph the Red Nosed Reindeer*, still in radio play. He used his nickname, Gene, as a stage name,[10] because of easy recognition. He was often called "The Singing Cowboy." After his career as a singer and actor ended, he turned to another passion – pro baseball. As well as purchasing TV and radio stations he bought a baseball team.

Lauren Bacall (September 16, 1924 – August 12, 2014) American actress
Birth Name – Betty Joan Perske

1945 Liberty Publications Photo,
Public Domain

Bacall was born in the Bronx, New York, the only child of Jewish parents, her mother being an immigrant from Romania. Her parents divorced while she was still a young girl, and she took her maternal grandmother's surname, Bacal,[11] also being used by her own mother. She later added another 'l' for clarity of pronunciation.

Educated by wealthy uncles in Brooklyn, she began her career as a model for **Howard Hawks**, whose secretary sent her to Hollywood for an audition because of a misunderstanding. As a result, she was selected as leading lady with **Humphrey Bogart** in *To Have and Have Not* (1944). Hawks signed her and changed her name to Lauren.[12] In her screen test she developed her famous trademark "look," ironically, because of her nerves. Her roles and relationship with Bogart in numerous films through the 1940s skyrocketed her to fame.

17

String Bean (June 17, 1915 – November 10, 1973) American banjo player, comedian, TV star
Birth Name -- David Akeman

1960s Publicity Photo (Fair Use)

Born in Annville, Kentucky to a father who played banjo at square dances, Akeman made his first instrument out of a shoebox, and at age 12 traded a pair of roosters for a real banjo. In a contest held by **Asa Martin**, who was looking for a banjo player, David won. Martin couldn't pronounce his last name so he introduced him as "String Beans."[13] He kept the stage name, later changing it to String Bean. He joined **Bill Monroe**'s group in 1943, where he teamed with **Willie Egbert Estbrook**. The two formed a comedy duo billed as "String Beans and Cousin Wilbur." After leaving Monroe and being replaced by **Lester Flatt**, he first began working with **Grandpa Jones** (also featured) then **Leo Childre**, with whom he became a regular on the Grand Ole Opry. He was one of the original members of the *Hee Haw* cast in 1969, where he remained until his untimely death. Upon returning from an Opry performance, he and his wife, Estelle were surprised by burglars who shot and killed them instantly.

Pat Benatar (January 10, 1953-_____) American singer and songwriter

Birth Name — Patricia Mae Andrzejewski (1979 Photo, Fair use)

Born in Brooklyn and reared on Long Island, Pat became interested in theater and singing at age eight, when she took voice lessons and sang her first solo at her elementary school. In senior high she participated in musical theater, playing Queen Guinevere in *Camelot*, and doing a solo of *The Christmas Song* on a choir recording in her senior year. With prior plans to attend Julliard, she surprised her family by her decision to pursue health education at the University of New York at Stony Brook instead. After her first year she dropped out to marry her first husband, army draftee, Dennis Benatar,[14] giving her the name by which she would go in her music career. While her husband was stationed at Fort Lee near Richmond, Virginia, she worked as a bank teller, a job which she quit to pursue music when inspired by a **Lisa Minnelli** concert. At first she worked as a singing waitress at a 1920s style nightclub, getting a gig in lounge band Coxon's Army, a regular at **Sam Miller**'s basement club, which became the subject of a PBS special, leading to stardom in the '80s.

Barbi Benton (January 28, 1950-_____) American model, actress and singer
Birth Name — Barbara Lynn Klein

1977 ABC Photo from *Sugar Time* (PD)

This popular "*Hee Haw* Honey" was propelled to stardom through her role on the show *Playboy After Dark* and subsequent appearances on the cover of *Playboy Magazine* and in nude layouts, originally in March, 1970 at age 20, at first credited as Barbi Klein. This was followed by features in several other issues up through December, 1985. During the first of the *Playboy* years, from 1969 through 1976, she was one of **Hugh Hefner's** girlfriend-mates. Hef soon convinced her to change her name to Barbi Benton.[15] During these years she also appeared as a regular cast member of *Hee Haw*, and attained a bit of success from a recording contract with one top five hit in 1975, *Brass Buckles*. All together she recorded eight albums. One of her recordings, *Ain't it Just That Way*, 1976, was a number one hit in Sweden for five weeks. In 2011, Hefner posted on Twitter that his best memory from *Playboy After Dark* was meeting Barbi.

She married in 1979 and has two children.

20

Bono (May 10, 1960-_____) Irish singer, songwriter, musician, businessman and philanthropist
Birth Name — Paul David Hewson

1980's Publicity Photo (Fair Use)

Bono was the shortened form of a nickname given to this star by a friend — *Bono Vox*, which means in Latin, "Good Voice."[16] That is certainly true of him!

Most people identify with him as the lead singer of the rock band, U2. Born and raised in Dublin, Bono attended Mount Temple Comprehensive School where he met **Allison Stewart**, destined to become his wife, as well as one of the future members of his iconic band. Bono writes the lion's share of U2 song lyrics using religious, political and social themes, which have contributed to the rebellious tone and attitude of the group's music. As time went on, many lyrics have been influenced by his personal experiences. He has done a number of benefit concerts and was granted honorary knighthood by **Queen Elizabeth II.**

21

The Big Bopper (October 24, 1930 – February 3, 1959) American musician, songwriter and disc jockey
Birth Name—Jiles Perry Richardson, Jr.

1950s Publicity Photo, Public Dom.

Being born in Sabine Pass, Texas, Richardson's family moved to Beaumont, where he graduated from high school in 1947. Later, while studying law at Lamar College, he was a member of the band and chorus, and played with the **Johnny Lampson Combo.** He worked part time at a radio station and quit college, getting married, having a daughter, and being promoted to Supervisor of Announcers at the station, WTRM. In 1955 he was drafted into the Army. In February, 1957, after making corporal, he was discharged and returned to WTRM. A sponsor wanted him to do a dance show. Usually called JP, he had seen college students doing a dance called the Bop, and decided to call himself "The Big Bopper."[17] He was a big hit, and began songwriting, writing *Running Bear* for **Johnny Preston.** He was signed by Mercury Records as a singer and hit with *Chantilly Lace* in 1958. He was killed with **Buddy Holley** and **Richie Valens** in the fatal plane crash which was called "The Day the Music Died" in **Don McLean's** *American Pie.*

22

(Lil) Bow Wow (March 9, 1987-_____) American rapper, actor and television host
Birth Name — Shad Gregory Moss

At Obama *We Are the Future* **Concert, 2009,** Public Domain

Originally rapping as Kid Gangsta, when this performer did a concert in Los Angeles, rapper **Snoop Dog** called him "Lil Bow Wow."[18] The handle stuck. He released his first album using that name in 2000 at only age 13, *Beware of Dog*, reminiscent of Snoop, followed by *Doggie Bag* in 2001. His third album, in 2003, *Unleashed*, credits him as simply Bow Wow. His next album, *Unwanted*, had a single, *Let Me Hold You*, featuring Omarion, which peaked at number one on the rap chart. He has released two more albums and is currently working on another, after signing with Cash Money Records.

Bow Wow appeared in a cameo in *All about the Benjamins* in 2002. This was followed the same year with a lead role in *Like Mike*. This led to a supporting role in *The Fast and the Furious: Tokyo Draft* in 2006, as well as appearances on the television series, *Entourage*.

23

Alison Brie (December 29, 1982-_____) American actress
Birth Name — Alison Schermmerhorn

IMDb Photo, Fair Use

Alison's father was of mixed European ancestry, and attended a sort of "Hindu-Christian hybrid church" to which she sometimes accompanied him in childhood. Alison's mother, however, was Jewish and wouldn't let her forget her heritage.

Her acting career started onstage at the Jewish Community Center in Los Angeles. She graduated from the California Institute of the Arts in 2005 with a bachelor's in theater then studied at the Royal Scottish Academy of Music and Drama in Glasgow. Soon, she was portraying a hairdresser on **Miley Cyrus'** popular young teen show, *Hannah Montana*. She went on to star in a Web Series, and was selected for the role of Trudy Campbell on *Mad Men*.

She changed her last name when she was young because it was often mispronounced and she felt that it had a terrible sound when it was.[19]

Charles Bronson (November 3, 1921 – August 30, 2003) American film and television actor
Birth Name – Charles Dennis Buckinsky

1966 Publicity Photo, Public Domain
Bronson was born in the Alleghany Mountain region of Pennsylvania, and much like **Nick Adams** and **Jack Palance**, was from a background of immigrant coal miners. His father was a Lithuanian immigrant and his mother's parents were also Lithuanian immigrants. Before learning English, Charles spoke Lithuanian and Russian at home. When he was 10 years old, his father died and he went to work in the coal mines, earning $1.00 for each ton of coal mined. Still, he graduated from high school and entered the Army Air Corp, serving in World War II in Guam, receiving a Purple Heart.

After the war he joined a theater group in Philadelphia, later sharing an apartment in New York with **Jack Klugman**. In 1950 he married and moved to Hollywood, enrolling in acting classes and picking up parts. In *You're in the Navy Now,* he was billed with his real name. In 1954, during the House of Un-American Activities proceedings, he changed his name to Bronson at the urging of his agent. [20] Big successes came from 1960 on.

25

Albert Brooks (July 22, 1947-_____) American actor, voice actor, writer, comedian and director
Birth Name — Albert Einstein

2011, Drive Premier,
Creative Commons Attribution

It doesn't take a genius to figure out why Albert changed his name (by age 19). He even jokes that he is the real **Albert Einstein**, and that he changed his name to sound more intelligent.[21]

Brooks, a Beverly Hills native, was reared in Pittsburg, where he attended Carnegie Mellon but dropped out to focus on his career. He received an Oscar in 1987 for his role in the film, *Broadcast News*. He is also the voice of Martin the clam fish in *Finding Nemo*, has done guest voice appearances on *The Simpsons*, and was in *The Simpsons Movie* as Russ Cargill. He has also written and stared in several hit films, not the least of which was *Defending Your Life*, a comedy which I greatly enjoyed, portraying a departed soul in the afterlife reflecting on his life on earth.

Mel Brooks (June 28, 1926-_____) American film director, screenwriter, comedian, actor, producer, songwriter and composer
Birth Name — Melvin Kaminsky

1970s Publicity Photo, Public Domain

Born in Brooklyn, NY, his father's family were German Jews from the Baltic seaport which is now Gdansk, Poland, and his mother's family were Ukrainian Jews from Kiev. He felt that Kaminsky was too ethnic because of the wave of anti-Semitism at time he entered his career, so he changed his name to Brooks.[22] He was angry over his father's death of kidney disease at his age two, and he took his new name from a modification of his mother's maiden name of Brookman.

Best known for producing numerous film farces and parodies, Brooks began his career in the "Borscht Belt" of the Catskill Mountains, then as a comic and writer, appearing on *Your Show of Shows*, an early 1950s television variety show, being paired with **Carl Reiner** in a comedy duo. In middle age, he became the most successful film director of the 1970s, eventually winning an Emmy, a Grammy and an Oscar. He was married to **Anne Bancroft** until her death in 2005.

Red Buttons (February 5, 1919 – July 13, 2006) American comedian and actor

Birth Name — Aaron Chwatt

1959 Publicity Photo, Public Domain

Born in New York City to Jewish immigrants, he went to work as an entertaining bellhop at Ryan's Tavern in the Bronx at age 16. His red hair and the large shiny buttons on his bell hop uniform gave orchestra leader Charles "Dinty" Moore the idea to call him "Red Buttons,"[23] the name which stuck with him throughout his career. Later that summer he worked as a comedian with **Robert Alda**, father of actor **Alan Alda** as his straight man, like **Mel Brooks**, in the resorts in the Catskill Mountains, popular with Jews from New York, colloquially called the Borscht Belt.

Drafted into the U.S. Army Air Forces, he appeared in their Broadway show, *Winged Victory,* with several future stars including **John Forsythe, Karl Mauldin** and **Lee J. Cobb**. He won an Oscar for Best Supporting Actor in *Sayonara* (1957) and played many other distinguished roles.

28

Nicolas Cage (January 7, 1964-_____) American actor and producer
Birth Name — Nicolas Kim Coppola

2013 Deauville Film Festival,
Georges Baird, Creative Commons Attribution-Share Alike

Born in Long Beach, California, a member of the famous Hollywood family and a nephew of legendary director, **Francis Ford Coppola**, Nic didn't want to appear to be taking advantage of nepotism, so he decided to change his surname. He was inspired, at least in part, to choose the name Cage by the comic superhero, Luke Cage.[24]

His minor role in *Fast Times at Ridgemont High* at age 18 began his career and since then he has appeared in a wide range of major roles from comedy to drama and even some offbeat films. He has been twice nominated for Oscars, winning once for his role as a suicidal alcoholic in the 1995 romantic drama *Leaving Las Vegas.*

Michael Caine (March 14, 1933) British Actor and author
Birth Name — Maurice Joseph Micklewhite

1960s Publicity Photo, Public Domain

Born in London, his father was a fish market porter and his mother a cook and charwoman. Growing up, his family lived in prefab housing with an outside toilet. He originally responded to an ad for an assistant stage manager. There he got small walk on parts. Originally wanting to use Michael Scott as a stage name, he was told that it was in use by another actor. Being pressed for a name selection by his agent on the phone, Caine noticed the movie showing at the nearby cinema and named himself after **Humphrey Bogart**'s character in "The Caine Mutiny."[25] Caine made his breakthrough in the 1960s when he had starring roles in acclaimed British films, including *Alfie* (1966), for which he was nominated for an Oscar. His most notable roles, however, came in the '70s in such films as *Sleuth* (1972), for which he received his second Oscar nomination, *The Man Who Would Be King* (1975) and *A Bridge Too Far* (1978). The '80s also brought acclaim to his work in movies such as *Educating Rita* (1983) which won him both a BAFTA and Golden Globe for Best Actor. He is highly recognized for his thick Cockney accent.

Truman Capote (September 30, 1924 – August 25, 1984) American author, screenwriter, playwright and actor
Birth Name—Truman Streckfus Persons

1959 Photo, *Roger Higgins*, PD

Born in New Orleans, his young parents divorced when he was four, and he spent the next five years with his mother's family in Mooreville, Alabama, bonding with a distant relative, Nanny Rumbley Faulk, whom Truman called "Sook." There he was a neighbor and friend of **Harper Lee**, author of *To Kill a Mockingbird*. Capote stated that the character of Dill in the book was based on him.

He taught himself to read before first grade, and began writing fiction by age 11. In 1932 he went to live with his mother and stepfather, Joe Capote, whose name he took,[26] in New York, later graduating from Franklin School, an Upper West Side private school. Then he went to work as a copyboy in the art department at The New Yorker, but his writing took time to meet success.

His most notable writings, both of which were made into powerful movies, are *Breakfast at Tiffany's* and *In Cold Blood*.

31

Lewis Carroll (27 January 1832 – 14 January 1898) English
writer, mathematician, logician, Anglican deacon and photographer
Birth Name — Charles Lutwidge Dodgson

1863 Photo, Public Domain

From a family of conservative army officers and Anglican clergy,
Dodgson was born in a small parsonage in Daresburg in Cheshire,
England. He was educated at home from a tot and by age seven he was
reading *Pilgrim's Progress*. Like most of his siblings he was troubled by
stuttering, making him less social. At 12 he was sent to Richmond
Grammar School, then Rugby School, where he was unhappy. Finally he
was sent to Oxford, where he became a member of his father's old
college, Christ Church. Right after entering Oxford he was notified that
his mother had died. He was also hampered by a fever which left him
deaf in one ear. In spite of his disadvantages he developed ability as a
storyteller and did charades. He spent time writing and published *Alice
in Wonderland* and other fantasy books and work, using the name, Lewis
Carroll, which he said was his "alter ego,"[27] making friends with other
writers. He was also an inventor and child photographer whose intent
was questionable.

Cyd Charisse (March 8, 1922 – June 17, 2008) American actress/dancer
Birth Name—Tula Ellice Finklea

1949 Publicity Photo, Public Domain

Born in Amarillo, Texas, to a jeweler father, she was diagnosed with polio as a young child and started taking dance lessons at age six to strengthen her legs. Her younger brother, Thomas, tried to call her Sis, and it came out Sid, giving her the nickname which was later changed to Cyd.[28] At age 12 she studied ballet in Los Angeles and at 14, she was accepted by Ballet Russe de Monte Carlo for the role of "Felia Siderova," and later, "Maria Istomina." During a European tour she met up again with dancer **Nico Charisse**, with whom she had studied in Los Angeles, and they were married. Returning to LA, she was offered a dancing role in *Something to Shout About*, bringing her to the attention of choreographer **Robert Alton**—who had also discovered **Gene Kelly**—and soon she joined the Freed Unit at MGM. She was paired **with Gene Kelly** and **Fred Astaire** (also featured) in dancing/acting roles in *Singin' in the Rain* (1952), *The Band Wagon* (1953) and *Silk Stockings* (1957). In 1992 she made her Broadway debut. In 2006 she was awarded the National Medal of the Arts and Humanities.

33

Charo (January 15, 1961-_____) Spanish-American actor, comedian and flamenco guitarist
Birth Name — María del Rosario Pilar Martínez Molina Baeza

2013 Alma Awards, *Richard Sandoval*, CCA

This feisty comedienne's official name is even larger than her birth name — María Rosario Pilar Martínez Molina Moquiere de les Esperades Santa Ana Romanguera y de la Najosa Rasten. Thus it is easy to see why she chose to shorten it to simply "Charo," for Rosario, which was her nickname as a child.[29] Charo is best known for her flamboyant stage antics, provocative outfits and her trademark warble.

Born in Muricia, Spain, her father fled to Casablanca for political asylum during the reign of Franco, while her mother stayed and raised their children. Charo studied guitar under **Andres Segovia** from age nine. Segovia said in an interview that he once told her, "Stop saying, 'cuchi-cuchi' so much, Charo! Be serious." After being discovered at an early age by famed 66-year-old band leader Xavier Cugat, she married him at only age 16, though her age was reported as 20. Shortly afterward she began appearing on U.S. TV shows like *The Today Show* and *Rowan and Martin's Laugh In*, and her career was off.

Chevy Chase (October 8, 1943-_____) American comedian, actor and writer
Birth Name — Cornelius Crane Chase

1960s Publicity Photo, Public Domain

Chase's grandmother called him "Chevy" as a nickname after a wealthy Maryland community,[30] and he chose it for his stage name. It is also from the traditional English song "The Ballad of Chevy Chase."

Born into an affluent family in New York, Chase worked at odd jobs before his career in comedy. His first role was in *National Lampoon's Vacation* films. Quickly he became a leading cast member of the first season of *Saturday Night Live*, which enforced his claim to being a household name. Other memorable roles include the classic *Caddyshack* (1980), *Fletch* (1985), *Spies Like Us* (1985) and *Three Amigos* (1986). He has twice hosted the Academy Awards, and was a regular cast member of NBCs *Community* from 2009 to 2012.

Jessica Chastain (March 24, 1977-_____) American actress
Birth Name—Jessica Michelle Howard (Biological, Monasterio)

2014 Deauville Film Fest., *Georges Biard*, CC

Jessica actually goes by her mother's maiden name.[31] This still makes her distantly related to me since all the Chastains in the U.S. are descended from the family of French Huguenot immigrant Dr. Pierre Chastain according to the family history, and I have two Chastain lines.

Born in Sacramento, California, she was reared by her mother and stepfather, Michael Hastey. She expressed an interest in acting at age seven when her grandmother took her to see a production starring **David Cassidy**. Though she struggled in high school and obtained an "adult diploma," she later attended Sacramento City College where she starred as Juliette in *Romeo and Juliette*, put on by *TheaterWorks*, a professional company in the bay area. A **Robin Williams** scholarship took her to Julliard in New York City, where she graduated in 2003. Shortly afterward she signed a TV deal with producer **John Wells**.

She gained wide recognition for several films, but received great critical acclaim for her role in *Zero Dark Thirty* in 2012.

Chubby Checker (October 3, 1941-_____) American singer-songwriter and dance trend setter
Birth Name — Ernest Evans

1960 Publicity Photo, Public Domain

Checker was born in Spring Gully, South Carolina and reared in the projects of South Philadelphia where he attended high school with, and became friends with, Fabiano Forte, who would become a popular singer under the name **Fabian**. After school he would entertain the customers at his jobs with songs and jokes, one of which was The Produce Market, where his boss gave him the nickname "Chubby." Another was at Fresh Farm Poultry, owned by Henry Colt. Colt was so impressed with the boy that he introduced him to a friend, **Kal Mann**, who worked as a songwriter for Cameo-Parkway Records. Mann arranged for him to do a private recording session for the legendary **Dick Clark** who was hosting *American Band Stand*. At the session, Clark's wife asked him his name. "Well, my friends call me 'Chubby,'" he answered. Chubby had just completed an impression of **Fats Domino**, so she smiled and said, "As in Checker?"[32] The play on words stuck.

Cher (May 20, 1946-_____) American singer, songwriter, actress, model, fashion designer, television host, comedian, dancer, business-woman, philanthropist, author, film producer, director, and record producer

Birth Name — Cherilyn Sarksian

1970s Publicity Photo, Public Domain

With a name which is a shortened form of her true first name,[33] this show business icon has so many facets to her career that it seems her talents are endless. She burst onto the scene in 1965 as half of the folk-rock husband-wife duo, **Sonny and Cher**. Their first hit, *I've Got You Babe* caught on like wildfire and plunged them onward to fame. Almost immediately Cher began a solo career with million-selling *Bang, Bang (My Baby Shot Me Down)* in 1966. Their anti-drug lifestyle lost them some of their popularity in the late '60's. Then in the 1970s they hit again with the *Sonny and Cher Comedy Hour*, gaining over 30 million viewers weekly. Then she had three number one hits. The couple divorced in 1975, and Cher once again had to start over, but the 1980s brought acclaim on Broadway and in movies like her Oscar nominated *Silkwood, Mask* and *Moonstruck*.

Patsy Cline (September 8, 1932 – March 5, 1963) American singer
Birth Name — Virginia Patricia Hensley

1957 Four Star Records, Public Dom.

Patsy was born in Gore, Virginia to a 16-year-old seamstress mother and 45-year-old blacksmith father. Soon having younger siblings, the family moved to Winchester and her father eventually left home. She began singing in church at an early age. At age 13 she contracted a throat infection and rheumatic fever. When she recovered, however, her voice was better than ever. Watching performers through the window of the radio station, she asked disc jockey **Jimmy McCoy** if she could sing on his show. This led to performances all around the tri-state area, where she wore fringed Western outfits which she designed and her mother made, and developed a wide following.

In 1952 she began to be managed by **Bill Peer**, who gave her the name Patsy from her middle name. On September 9, 1953 she married contractor Gerald Cline. Although they divorced, she kept the name.[34] In 1954, **Jimmy Dean** learned about her and made her a regular on *Connie B. Gay's Town and Country Jubilee* in Arlington. In 1955 she signed with Decca Records. She became a great influence on country music. She died in a plane crash in 1963 with two other stars, at only 30 years of age.

Alice Cooper (February 4, 1948-_____) American singer, songwriter and musician
Birth Name: Vincent Damon Furnier

1960s Promo Photo, Public Domain

Born in Detroit, Michigan, the son of a lay preacher with the Church of Jesus Christ, traditionally a branch of the Latter Day Saints, he was named for one of his uncles, Vincent Collier Furnier, and writer **Damon Runyon**. His paternal grandfather was actually an "Apostle" in the Church of Jesus Christ. Following a series of childhood illnesses, he moved with his family to Phoenix, Arizona, where he attended high school and community college. In 1964, at age 16, he eagerly participated in a talent contest, gathering teammates to compete. The group chose the name the Earwigs. Unable to play instruments, they dressed up like the **Beatles** and mimicked their singing, and won the contest. They changed their name to the Spiders and featured Furnier on vocals. They made their first record in 1967. They reportedly took the name Alice Cooper from a Ouiji board, allegedly conveying the spirit of a 16th century witch.[35] Stage shows featured blood, snakes, etc. He took the name forward into his solo career. The music was called "Shock Rock."

Gary Cooper (May 7, 1901 – May 13, 1961) American film actor
Birth Name — Frank James Cooper

1936 Promo Photo, Public Domain

Born and educated in Montana, Cooper's family moved to Los Angeles, California in the fall of 1924 when his father left his post on the Montana Supreme Court Bench. He joined them on Thanksgiving Day.

After odd jobs, Cooper met with Montana friends Jim Galeen and Jim Callaway who were working as film extras and stunt riders in B Westerns. He decided to join them, and began his career in pictures in 1925 doing stunt roles in with **Tom Mix** making $5.00 a day. Wanting to get past this and into real acting parts, he paid for a screen test then hired casting director **Nan Collins** as his agent. Because other actors were using the name **Frank Cooper**, Collins suggested changing his name to Gary after Collins' hometown of Gary, Indiana. He agreed, liking the name right off the bat.[36] His career spanned 35 years. His memorable roles include *A Farewell to Arms* (1932), *Meet John Doe* (1941), *Sergeant York* (1941), *For Whom the Bell Tolls* (1943) and *High Noon* (1952).

41

Cowboy Copas (July 15, 1913 – March 5, 1963) American country music singer

Birth Name— Lloyd Estel Copas

1960s Grand Ole Opry Photo, Public Domain

Born in Blue Creek, Ohio, this "Country Gentleman of Song" began performing locally at age 14, appearing on WLW and WKRC-AM radio in Cincinnati during the 1930s. Moving to Knoxville, Tennessee in 1940, he began singing on WNOX-AM with his band, the Gold Star Rangers. Previously known as Natchee the Indian, he acquired Cowboy as his stage name because of his soft Western style and dress.[37]

In 1943 he achieved national recognition by replacing **Eddie Arnold** in the **Pee Wee King Band** and performing on the *Grand Ole Opry*. His first single, *Flamingo Baby*, on King Records in 1946, made number 4 on the *Billboard Country Chart* and started his upward climb in success. His top hits included *Signed, Sealed and Delivered*, *Tennessee Waltz* and *'Tis Sweet to Be Remembered*.

Copas was killed in the plane crash near Camden, Tennessee, which also took the lives of **Patsy Cline** and **Hawkshaw Hawkins** (both featured).

David Copperfield (September 16, 1956-_____) American illusionist

Birth Name — David Seth Kotkin

2014 Photo, *Homer Liwag,* Public Domain

Born in Metuchen, New Jersey of Jewish parents, David went to a camp as a young child, which he sees as the experience that changed his life. He began practicing magic at age 10 as Divino, the Boy Magician, and was the youngest ever to be admitted to the *Society of American Magicians* at age 12.

At age 18, he enrolled in New York City's Fordham University, but three weeks into his freshman year he left school to play the lead role in the musical, *The Magic Man* in Chicago. At that time he adapted his stage name from **Charles Dickens'** famous novel, though thinking it too dark.[38] By age 19 he was headlining at the Pagoda Hotel in Honolulu, Hawaii. He was discovered by **Joseph Cates**, a Broadway and TV producer who produced a magic special for ABC in 1977, the first of many hosted by Copperfield. He has been hailed by *Forbes* as the most commercially successful magician in history.

Elvis Costello (August 25, 1954-_____) English singer-songwriter
Birth Name — Declan Patrick McManus

Publicity Photo, Public Domain

Born in Liverpool, England, to a musician and band leader father of Irish heritage, his first broadcast was with his dad in a TV commercial. His father used the stage name **Day Costello**, and he chose first to be called D.P. Costello.[39]

He did a demo tape and was signed to Stiff Records, and his manager, **Jake Riviera**, suggested he combine **Elvis Presley**'s first name with Costello. His first single, *Less than Zero* was released March 25, 1977 and less than four months later his critically acclaimed debut album, *My Aim is True*, came out.

Later Costello was signed by CBS's Columbia Records label. He is largely associated with the first wave of British punk, and his later albums took him to the top. His first three albums all appeared in *Rolling Stone*'s list of the 500 Greatest Albums of All Time. He is also an avid fan of country music.

Joan Crawford (March 23, 1904-May 10, 1977) American film and television actress
Birth Name — Lucille Fay LeSueur

1936 Publicity Photo, *George Hurrell*, P.D.

Likely the child of unwed parents, and an absentee father, Crawford had a troubled childhood. She was born in San Antonio, Texas. Her mother later married Henry Cassin who ran an opera house in Lawton, Oklahoma. Vaudeville performers of the day played there, and Crawford dreamed of being a dancer. Later, they moved to Kansas City and Cassin placed her in St. Agnes Academy. Then after attending Rockford and Stephens College, she dropped out.

Under her own name she began dancing in choruses and was spotted by producer **Jacob J. Shubert**, who put her in a chorus line for *Innocent Eyes*. She did a screen test and was offered a job with MGM. Credited as Lucille LeSueur in *Lady of the Night* (1924), after **Pete Smith** realized her star quality, he placed a contest in *Movie Weekly* called "Name the Star," out of which emerged her stage name, which she actually did not like![39]

Tom Cruise (July 3, 1962-_____) American actor, filmmaker and Scientologist

Birth Name — Thomas Cruise Mapother IV

2014, *Georges Biard*, Creative Commons

Born on the 3rd of July, not the 4th, like his famous movie, his ancestral family name was actually O'Mara. That was changed by his great-grandfather. But "Tom Cruise" is just dropping his surname altogether. Cruise was actually the surname of one of his paternal third great grandfathers. He was raised in near poverty in a family of four children dominated by his abusive father. Born in Syracuse, New York, Cruise spent part of his childhood in Canada, where his dad worked as a consultant with the Canadian Armed Forces. Briefly attending a Franciscan Seminary in Cincinnati, he aspired to be a priest.

His first film appearance was a bit part in *Endless Love* in 1981, quickly followed by a supporting role in *Taps*. He changed his name at the request of his first agent, **Tobe Gibson**.[40] *Risky Business* (1983) took him really into a leading role, and then *Top Gun* (1986) made him a superstar.

Miley Cyrus (November 23, 1992) American singer, songwriter and actress
Birth Name — Destiny Hope Cyrus

2112 People's Choice, *JJ Duncan*, C.C.

Born in Franklin, Tennessee, the daughter of country music star, **Billy Ray Cyrus**, Miley, originally Smiley, because she smiled so much, was her childhood nickname.[41] After minor roles on her dad's show, *Doc*, she got her big break in the role of Disney Channel teen idol, *Hannah Montana*. In 2007 she signed a record deal with Hollywood Records and released her first album, *Meet Miley Cyrus*. After being certified as quadruple platinum, it was followed up by the hit single, *See You Again*.

In spite of her metamorphosis from benign teen image to naughty girl, her fame has continued to accelerate, and surprisingly, much with those who idolized her in the Hannah Montana role. Her film career launched as a voice actress in the animated film, *Bolt* (2008), and the following year she starred in the feature film, *Hannah Montana, the Movie*, in which one of my granddaughters was an extra. The soundtrack featured the hit song, *Climb*, which typified Cyrus' own changed role.

Doris Day (April 3, 1922-_____) American actress and singer
Birth Name — Doris Mary Ann Kappelhoff

1957 Publicity Photo, Public Domain

Though she has given her birth year as 1924, census records show her as being 18 years of age in 1940, placing the year of birth at 1922. She was born in Cincinnati, Ohio, and had two older brothers. Her parents separated and she became interested in dance, forming a duo with **Jerry Doherty**. Her legs were injured in an auto accident, which left her unable to continue in this vein. While recovering she began singing along with the Big Bands on the radio, and discovered another talent. She was inspired by **Ella Fitzgerald**. Her mother then gave her lessons and her teacher told her that Doris had great potential. That teacher, **Grace Raine**, had much influence on her style. She was hired by radio station WLW for Carlin's Carnival show, and in a restaurant. On the show she caught the attention of **Barney Rapp** who chose her for a job. While working for him she changed her surname to "Day" at his suggestion because Kappelhoff did not fit marquees.[42] She went on to star in many movies and to have her own TV vehicle, *The Doris Day Show*.

Sandra Dee (April 13, 1942 –February 20, 2005) American Actress
Birth Name: Alexandra Zuck

1960s Publicity Photo, Public Domain

Born in Bayonne, New Jersey, Dee was the only child of Russian Orthodox parents who divorced when she was only five years old. She began modeling at four years old, and at the age of eight, began to go by Sandra (Short for Alexandra) Douvan (her stepfather's name). She progressed first to television commercials. The studios renamed her Sandra Dee when her movie career started in the late 1950s, [43] Always playing virginal roles, she once said she was the junior **Doris Day** for years.

Her first film was *Until They Sail* in 1957. She won a Golden Globe in 1959 as one of the most promising newcomers in films. She starred in *Gidgit*, with **Cliff Robertson**, *Imitation of Life* with **Lana Turner** and **John Gavin**, *Tammy Tell Me True* with **Stefanie Powers** and **Gina Lollobrigida** and in *Come September* with **Bobby Darin**, whom she married in 1960. Her popularity began to decline by 1967 after her highly publicized divorce from Darin. She died of complications of kidney disease at the age of 62.

Delilah (February 15, 1960-_____) American radio personality, author, actress and songwriter
Birth Name — Delilah Rene Luke

CNN Photo, Pinterest, Fair Use

Born in North Bend, Oregon, this "Queen of Sappy Love Songs," who chooses to go by her first name on-air to protect hers and her family's privacy and security,[44] gives advice to the lovelorn on her adult contemporary syndicated coast-to-coast radio show aimed at young to middle-aged adults. However, her personal life has been riddled with problems and conflicts. She has been married four times and divorced three. She and her current husband, Paul, were married at her home in 2012. She has 3 natural and several adopted African children, and founded a non-profit humanitarian organization, Point Hope, in Ghana. One adopted child, Sammy Rene, died in 2012 from sickle cell anemia.

A conservative Christian, she plays songs and gives advice, which she sees as practical, to callers which are not allowed to disclose their locations. Her show has an estimated eight million listeners. She lives near Port Orchard, Washington, where she owns and operates a restaurant. She has written three books.

Lana Del Rey (June 21, 1985-_____) American singer, songwriter
Birth Name — Elizabeth Grant

2012 Canes Film Fest., *Georges Biard*, C.C.

Born in New York City to affluent parents, she grew up in Lake Placid. She dealt with alcohol dependence in Kent School in Connecticut. There, a friend, Gene Campbell, a young teacher, exposed her to music and pop culture on weekend drives, inspiring her song, *Boarding School*. She later attended Fordham University studying philosophy and metaphysics.

She sang in her church choir as a child, and her uncle taught her guitar at 18. She performed in night clubs under other names, one of which was her own: Lizzy Grant. In April 2005, she recorded a 7 tract CD. The album *Sirens* was released in 2006 under the name May Jailer. These names failed to result in a successful star. That year she met **Van Wilson**, a rep for 5 Point Records, at the Williamsburg Live Songwriting Competition, and signed a deal in 2007 while still at Fordham. Her stage name was decided by lawyers and managers.[45] Her debut album, *Lana Del Rey* came out in 2008.

John Denver (December 31, 1943 – October 12, 1997) American Pop-Folk singer and musician
Birth Name—Henry John Deutschendorf, Jr.

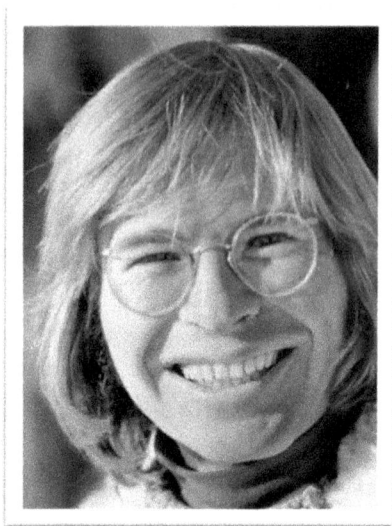

1973 TV Promo Photo, Public Domain

Early in his career, John insisted on using his father's name, however, when playing in Denver with the **New Christie Minstrels**, of which his uncle Dave Deutschendorf was a member, he was told that he must change his name. Frankly, the long name wouldn't fit on the marquis. Having recorded a song titled *Denver*, and his music reflecting the mood of the area, Denver was chosen as his stage name.[46]

He became the most popular pop star of the early 1970s with numerous top hits charting in both adult contemporary and country genres, like *Take Me Home, Country Roads* (1971), *Rocky Mountain High* (1972) and *Annie's Song* (1974).

Denver was killed when his experimental Rutan Long-EZ Plane crashed into Monterey Bay off the California coast.

Portia de Rossi (January 31, 1973-_____) Australian actress, model and philanthropist
Birth Name — Amanda Lee Rogers

2007 Red Carpet
Photo, *Pulicanno*, Flikr, altered, Creative Commons Attribution- Share Alike

Born in Victoria, Australia, de Rossi was brought up by her mother after her father's death at her age nine. Modeling for print and television commercials as a child, this openly gay singer changed her name legally at age 15 due to her struggle with her sexual identity. Being a Shakespeare fan, she explains, she adapted Portia from *The Merchant of Venice*,[47] because she felt that an exotic Italian name would suit her better.

She got her first significant role playing a model in the Australian film, *Sirens*, in 1994. Soon afterward she moved to Los Angeles. She is best known for her roles as Nelle Porter on the TV series, *Ally McBeal*, and Lindsay Funk on the sitcom *Arrested Development*. She has struggled with anorexia, and says that her love for **Ellen DeGeneres**, to whom she is married, saved her from this.

Bo Derek (November 20, 1956- _____) American film and television actress, movie producer, and model
Birth Name — Mary Cathleen Collins

1970s Publicity Photo, Public Domain

Cathleen, as she was called, was born in Long Beach, California, and after her parents divorced, her mother, a makeup artist for **Ann Margaret**, married American stunt performer, **Bobby Bass**. Dropping out of high school without her mother's permission, she spent a lot of time on the beach surfing and sunbathing.

Caught by her disgruntled mom, she started back to school then left again with **John Derek** (see next page), a married actor/director thirty years her senior, with whom she had become romantically involved. John soon divorced his wife, actress **Linda Evans**, and married Cathleen in Germany. Immediately John started getting his young wife into films under the stage name Bo Derek.[48] She quickly became a sex symbol as she was portrayed that way in her roles in *Fantasies,* filmed in the summer of 1973 in Greece, not released until 1981, *Orca* (1977) and *10* in 1979.

54

John Derek (August 12, 1926 – May 22, 1998) American actor, director and photographer
Birth Name — Derek Delevan Harris

1956 Publicity Photo, Public Domain

Derek was born into the show business, so to speak, in Hollywood, the son of actor and director **Lawson Harris** and actress **Delores Johnson**. His noticeable good looks and his family connections put him in the enviable position to be groomed as a star even before age 18. To his chagrin, however, he was drafted into the U.S. Army in 1944 and served in the Philippines near the conclusion of World War II.

After the war, he contacted **Humphrey Bogart** who gave him his stage name [49] and cast him as a pretty-boy killer, Nick Romano, in *Knock on Any Door* (1949). His character action garnered his good reviews in the *New York Times*, and he was immediately cast as **Broderick Crawford**'s son in *All the King's Men* that same year, which won the Oscar for Best Picture. Other great roles followed. Then his fast play with ladies landed him in trouble when he latched onto **Bo** (see entry, previous page).

Dido (December 25, 1941-_____) English singer, songwriter
Birth Name — Florian Cloud de Bounevialle Armstrong

Hollywood Stroller Blog Photo, Fair Use

Born at St. Mary Abbott's Hospital in Kensington, London, England on Christmas Day, Dido is actually her parents' pet name for the singer. She was irritated by the fact that they named her such a complex name and then chose to call her something else. She said Florian was a German man's name, though (*so Dido must be better*), so she had it legally changed. Dido was the mythical Queen of Carthage.[50] Her older brother is famous record producer, **Rollo Armstrong**.

She was educated at Thornhill Primary School in Islington, Dallington School, City of London Girls' and Westminster School. At the latter she was taught contemporary music by **Sinan Savaskan**. Her early recordings in 1995 and '96 were co-written by her brother, Rollo. Her real breakthrough came in 1999 when the label to which she was signed was sold to BMG Records, and her debut album, *No Angel*, was released.

Vin Diesel (July 18, 1967-_____) American actor and filmmaker
Birth Name — Mark Sinclair Vincent

2009 Photo, *Andre Luis*;

Born in New York City and reared by his mother, Sherleen Sinclair (Vincent) and stepfather, **Irving H. Vincent**, an acting instructor and theater manager. He has never seen his biological father, but he took pride in his African-American heritage.

He made his first stage appearance at age seven in a children's play produced in Greenwich Village. Remaining in theater, he attended Hunter College and became involved in screenwriting. He changed his name to Vin Diesel while working as a bouncer in a night club in New York City. The name "Vin," he said, was short for Vincent, and "Diesel" was chosen because his friends said he ran off of diesel fuel because of his non-stop energy.[51] He is best known for his roles in *Saving Private Ryan* (**Stephen Spielberg**, 1998); *The Chronicles of Riddick* trilogy (2001-2013) and *The Fast and the Furious* film series (2001 to date), in which he was also a producer.

Franklin W. Dixon (October 25, 1902 – September 6, 1977)
Canadian author, journalist, screenwriter and filmmaker
Birth Name — Leslie McFarlane

Publicity Photo, Public Domain

Though the penname Franklin W. Dixon was used by later writers of *Hardy Boys* mystery books, McFarlane was the originator of both the books and the name.[52] The son of a school principal, he was brought up in the town of Haileybury, Ontario, Canada. He became a freelance writer shortly after high school, moving to Whitby in 1936, which he wrote about in *A Kid in Haileybury* (1975). As a young man he worked as a reporter in Ontario then took a job at the *Springfield Republican* in Massachusetts.

While in the U.S. he replied to an ad by the Stratemeyer Syndicate, publisher of *Nancy Drew* and the *Bobbsey Twins,* then freelanced as one of their authors using the pseudonym Roy Rockwood, writing seven *Dave Fearless* serialized mystery novels. Then he wrote 21 *Hardy Boys* books using Franklin W. Dixon as well as *Dana Girls* books using Carolyn Keene.

Snoop Dogg / Snoopzilla (October 20, 1971-_____) American rapper, singer-songwriter and actor
Birth Name — Cordozar Calvin Broadus Jr.

2013 Photo, India, altered, Creative Com.

Snoop was actually named after his stepfather, now deceased. His biological father, Vernall Varnado, a singer and mailman, was not even around before the divorce of Snoop's parents in 1975. As a youth he began singing in church and playing piano and was rapping by 6th grade. Though he graduated from high school, he became a gang member who clashed with the law in Long Beach, California, where the family lived and he soon was arrested for cocaine possession and was in and out of jail. While out, he and two cousins recorded homemade tapes as a group named **213** for the Long Beach area code. One of his early solos made it onto a mix tape and was discovered by **Dr. Dre** who invited him to an audition by phone. When he began recording in 1992, he took the stage name Snoop Doggie Dog, later shortened to Snoop Dogg. His starting band became known as The Dogg Pound. Several albums reflected the name, starting with his debut, *Doggystyle,* then *The Dogfather, No Limit Top Dog* and *Doggumentary.* His record company was named Doggy Style Records. In 2013 he changed it to Snoopzilla.[53]

Kirk Douglas (December 9, 1916-_____) American actor, producer and author
Birth Name — Issur Danielovitch

1969 Publicity Photo, Public Domain

Douglas was born in Amsterdam, New York of impoverished Russian Jewish immigrant parents, and the family spoke Yiddish at home. His father's brother had immigrated earlier, and adopted the name Dempsey, which the rest of the family did later. Kirk grew up as Izzy Dempsey, but changed his name to Kirk Douglas before entering the Navy during World War II.[55]

In his autobiography, *The Ragman's Son*, published in 1988, Douglas recalls: "My father, who had been a horse trader in Russia, got himself a horse and a small wagon, and became a ragman, buying old rags, pieces of metal, and junk for pennies, nickels, and dimes..." He made his film debut in *The Strange Love of Martha Ivers* in 1946 playing alongside **Barbara Stanwyck**, and soon was a leading box office star for over two decades, having a 90-film career spanning sixty years. He had three Oscar nominations, and achieved one for Lifetime Achievement, plus winning the Medal of Freedom.

Mike Douglas (August 11, 1920 – August 11, 2006) American Big Band era singer, entertainer and music/talk show host
Birth Name – Michael Delaney Dowd, Jr.

1956 Publicity Photo, Public Dom.

Born in Chicago, Mike began singing as a choir boy, and by his teens was entertaining on a cruise ship in Lake Michigan. After serving in the U.S. Army during World War II, he was a staff singer for WMAQ in Chicago; then moved to Los Angeles. After singing on a radio show he joined **Kay Kyser**, who gave him his stage name,[56] as a Big Band singer. In 1950 Mike was the voice of Prince Charming on **Walt Disney's** classic animated film, *Cinderella*. Kyser retired for health reasons in 1951, and big band style music became less marketable as rock and roll came to be.

However, in 1961 he moved to Cleveland, starting the afternoon television music and talk variety show known as *The Mike Douglas Show*, and from then until 1982 Mike reached his height of fame. He featured ballad and big band style singing, musicians, comedy, political personalities and sports figures. A pioneer in this field, he did 6,000 shows, most of which were an hour and a half in length, viewed in as many as 230 cities at one time. His show resonated a polite atmosphere when some others did not, setting him aside as a uniquely likable host.

Bob Dylan (May 24, 1941-_____) American singer-songwriter, trendsetter, artist and writer
Birth Name — Robert Allen Zimmerman

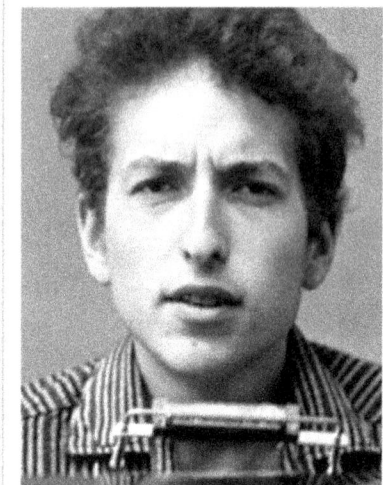

1960s Publicity Photo, Public Domain

Bob was born Duluth, Minnesota the grandson of Ukrainian Jewish immigrants, and Lithuanian Jewish immigrants. During his childhood he listened first to blues and country music on Shreveport, Louisiana stations, then as a teen to rock and roll. In high school he formed several bands, performing the songs of **Little Richard** and **Elvis Presley**.

He began using the pseudonym Elston Gunn, even performing with **Bobby Vee**. By college he was introducing himself as "Bob Dylan,"[57] performing on the Dinky town folk music circuit. He told his biographer, **Robert Shelton** that he wanted to make sure people knew he did not take his name from poet **Dylan Thomas**. Dillon was his mother's maiden name.[2] In May, 1960, he dropped out of college and went to New York the next January to perform and meet his idol, **Woody Guthrie**, who was ill. In September a review in the *New York Times* brought him to the attention of producer **John Hammond**, who signed him to Columbia Records. He has been one of the greatest influences on American music in history, winning numerous awards.

George Elliot (22 November 1819 – 22 December 1880) English novelist, journalist, and translator
Birth Name — Mary Ann Evans

1864 Portrait by *William Burton*

Mary Ann or Marian, as she was sometimes called, was born on the South Farm of Asbury Hill Estate in Warwickshire, which her father managed. She was intelligent and an avid reader, but plain in looks, so her father gave her a better education than most girls, sending her to boarding school at a young age where she was exposed to a religious evangelical atmosphere. After her mother's death the family moved to Coventry, where, in the home of Charles Bray, she met and became acquainted with free-thinkers like **Herbert Spencer** and **Ralph Waldo Emerson**.

Later she moved to London and met married philosopher, **George Lewes**, with whom she lived, and she began researching and writing. Her first publication was in the *Westminster Review* in 1856. She chose to write under a male name so her work would be taken more seriously.[58] Her greatest work was *Silas Marner* (1861), which is now available through *St. Clair Publications Classics*.

Carmen Electra (April 20, 1972-_____) American glamour model, actress, TV personality, singer and dancer
Birth Name—Tara Leigh Patrick

2113 © *Glen Francis,* www.PacificProDigital.com

Carmen was born in Sharonville, Ohio, the youngest of six children. As a young girl she studied under **Gloria J. Simpson** at Dance Artists Studio. At age nine she was enrolled in the School for Creative and Performing Arts in Cincinnati. There she was a classmate of **Nick Lachey** with whom she appeared in a production of *Peter Pan*. Later she graduated from Barbizon Modeling and Acting School in Cincinnati.

She began her career as a dancer at *King's Island*, an amusement park in Mason, Ohio. After meeting **Prince** in California in 1991, Carmen settled on her stage name, which she got from Prince,[59] before signing a record contract. She began appearing in TV shows in 1995. Then in 1997 she appeared in the first of several nude pictorials in *Playboy* magazine, leading to her role on *Baywatch*. She has been romantically linked to heavy metal stars **Tommy Lee** and **Freddy Durst**, and has appeared in several movies.

Dale Evans (October 31, 1912 – February 7, 2001) American writer, film star and singer-songwriter
Birth Name—Lucille Wood Smith

1940s Promo Photo, Public Domain

Born in Uvalde, Texas, Dale was named Lucille Wood Smith at birth and her name was changed to Francis Octavia Smith while still a small child. She had a troubled childhood, and eloped with Thomas F. Fox at age 14, giving birth to a son, Thomas F. Fox, Jr. at 15. A year later the couple was separated and she moved to Memphis, Tennessee as a single mother. Pursuing a career in music, she went to work at radio stations WMC and WREK where she sang and played piano. After her divorce, while briefly at WHAS, the station manager, Joe Eaton, gave her the name Dale Evans to promote her singing career.[60]

After two more failed marriages, in 1947 she married **Roy Rogers** in Davis, Oklahoma on the Flying L Ranch where they had filmed the movie *Home in Oklahoma*. It was Roy's second marriage and it lasted till Roger's death in 1998. Though they had only one child together, who died, he had some natural children, and they both had adopted ones, four together. They left a great legacy.

65

Linda Evans (November 18, 1942-_____) American actress
Birth Name — Linda Evanstad

1960s

Promo Photo, Public Domain

Born in Hartford, Connecticut as the second daughter of the grandson of immigrants from Evanstad, Norway, her family moved to Hollywood, California when she was six months old. Because of her shyness, her teacher insisted that she take drama at school. She took the name of Linda Evans as a teen even before beginning her career.[61]

Her first starring role was in *Bachelor Father* before her 18th birthday in 1960 which starred **John Forsythe**, with whom she would co-star twenty years later in *Dynasty*. After several guest roles in TV Westerns, she got her first regular part in 1965 with **Barbara Stanwyck** in the *Big Valley*.

She was first married to **John Derek** (also featured) who left her for Bo. Then she married property director, **Stan Herman**. After their divorce she began a relationship with musician, **Yanni**.

Morgan Fairchild (February 3, 1950-_____) American actress
Birth Name — Patsy Ann McClenny

© *Glenn Frances* www.PacificProDigital.com

Born in Dallas, Texas, Morgan's mother was a high school teacher. This popular actress began her journey early, appearing with **Jerry Haynes** on a local TV children's show as a young child then in the audience of the same station's bandstand show as a teen, auditioning three times to be a member of *The Little Group*, the show's dance ensemble. At the same time she appeared in several television commercials at various local stations.

Her first acting job was as a double for **Fay Dunaway** in *Bonnie and Clyde* (1967). She took her first name, Morgan, from the 1966 film, *Morgan: A Suitable Case for Treatment*,[62] starring **David Warner** and **Vanessa Redgrave**, and "Fairchild" could have referred to her early start. Her first on-screen role in *Search for Tomorrow* came after moving to New York beginning in 1973. She relocated in Los Angeles in 1977. After several other small parts, she landed the unforgettable role of Jenna Wade in *Dallas*. Many TV and movie roles followed.

67

Minnesota Fats (January 19, 1913 – January 18, 1996) American professional pockets billiards player/ hustler
Birth Name — Rudolf Walter Wanderone, Jr.

1960s Photo, Public Domain

Wanderone, originally called "New York Fats," actually adapted the name "Minnesota Fats" from the fictional character in Walter Travis' novel, *The Hustler*, made into a 1961 movie, which he claimed was actually based on his own persona.[63] Born in Brooklyn, NY, he hung around pool halls as a teen before he began traveling across the country in the late 1920s as a pool hustler. He was a showman all of his life, challenging entire poolrooms full of players, pretending that others were trying to hustle him. He would cry for mercy from his victims before taking all of their cash in bets.

Truly a legend in his own time, and a great story teller, Wanderone died in Nashville, Tennessee the day before his 83rd birthday of congestive heart failure. He was the self-proclaimed "Best pool player of all times."

68

Fergie Duhamel (March 27, 1975-_____) American singer, songwriter, fashion designer, television host, and actress
Birth Name — Stacy Ann Ferguson

2009, *Moses*, Creative Commons- Share Alike

Stacy was born in Hacienda Beach, California to devout Roman Catholic school teacher parents. She attended public high school where she was a straight-A student, a spelling bee champion and a Girl Scout.

She studied dance and began doing voiceover work for Sally on *Peanuts* cartoon specials for TV, and starred in the TV show, *Kids Incorporated* from 1984-1989. For ten years, beginning in 1992, she was a member of the female trio *Wild Orchid*.

Beginning in 1993 she attained great success as a member of **Black Eyed Peas**. Then her debut solo album, *The Duchess*, was released in September, 2006. Her songs have charted as high as number five on the Billboard Hot 100 and she has won various awards. Her original stage name, Fergie, was derived from a shortening of her Scottish surname, but in 2013, she decided to start using her married name as a part of her stage name.[64]

Flavor Flav (March 16, 1959-_____) American rapper, musician, actor and television personality and comedian
Birth Name — William Jonathan Drayton, Jr.

2011 *Stewart Sevastos*, Public Enemy- Creative Commons- Share Alike

Drayton was born and grew up in the town of Hempstead, New York, and was playing piano at age five. Seen as a child prodigy, he began singing in the youth choir at his church, mastering multiple musical instruments as a child. He had several scrapes with the law and was in and out of jail growing up.

In 1978 he graduated from culinary school and has cooked at several restaurants. He attended Adelphi College where he met Carlton Ridenhour, later known as **Chuck D**. He took the stage name Flavor Flav from his graffiti tag,[65] and collaborated with **Chuck D.** on his hip hop college radio show, and began rapping with him.

Flavor Flav came to prominence as a founding member of hip hop band, **Public Enemy**, on Def Jam Records. After a marginal first album the group's second release, *It Takes a Nation of Millions to Hold Us Back* went double platinum in 1988.

Gerald Ford (July 14, 1913 – December 26, 2006) 38th President of the United States
Birth Name—Leslie Lynch King, Jr.

Photo *David H. Kennedy*, Public Domain

Born in Omaha, Nebraska to a wool trader who was the son of a prominent banker, his mother, Dorothy, née Gardner, left his father sixteen days after his birth, taking him first to Oak Park, Illinois to the home of her sister, and then to live with her parents, Levi Addison Gardner and Adele Augusta Ayer in Grand Rapids, Michigan. After their divorce, his mother gained full custody. On January 1, 1916, she remarried Gerald Rudolf Ford, and called the boy Gerald Rudolph Ford, Jr. He was never formally adopted and didn't legally change his name until December 3, 1935, at that time adapting the more accepted spelling of his middle name.[66]

Ford played football and was a member of Delta Kappa Epsilon at the University of Michigan, where he washed dishes to help pay for school.

He was the first person ever appointed to the office of Vice President under the terms of the 25th amendment, upon the resignation of **Spiro Agnew**, and the first person to become both Vice President and President without being elected when **Richard Nixon** resigned.

Jodie Foster (November 19, 1962-_____) American actress, film director and producer
Birth Name — Alicia Christian Foster

JodyFosterCesars2011Cropped, GB

Born in Los Angeles, California, Foster was the youngest of four children of a former decorated U.S. Lt. Col., real estate broker from a wealthy family, who left Jody's mother before her birth. Her mother, Brandy, worked in public relations with Arthur P. Jacobs, a film producer. A gifted child, she learned to read before age three. She attended a French prep school, graduating in 1980 as valedictorian of the French division, then Yale with a BA in literature in 1985.

She was nicknamed Jodie by her three older siblings.[67] Her first role was at age three. Credit spellings changed a couple of times before the current spelling. She was credited in *Gunsmoke* in 1969 as Jody then in *Daniel Boone* in 1970 she was Jodi. Since then all credits have been as Jodie Foster. She had a more significant part as a child prostitute in *Taxi Driver* (1976) at age 15 for which she received an Oscar nomination for Best Supporting Actress. She received her first Oscar for Best Actress in 1989 for portraying a rape victim in *The Accused*, her second for *Silence of the Lambs* (1991) and a third nomination for *Nell* (1994).

Michael J. Fox (June 9, 1961-_____) Canadian-American actor, author and producer (noted for courageous handling of Parkinson's)
Birth Name — Michael Andrew Fox

1982 Universal Photo, fair use

Fox was born in Edmonton, Alberta, Canada, and his mother was a part time actress, which sparked his interest in acting. At age 15 he got his first role in *Leo and Me* produced by the CBC. In 1979, at age 18, he moved to Los Angeles to further his acting career. He was discovered by **Ronald Shedlo** who gave him his first U.S. role on *Letters from Frank*, a television film, where he was credited as Michael Fox. He discovered another actor by that name, and had to come up with an alteration. According to his autobiography, *A Lucky Man: A Memoir*, he didn't like the sound of Andrew so he decided to change his middle initial to J. in honor of actor **Michael J. Pollard**[68] who starred in *Bonnie and Clyde* (1967).

After a few film parts, he was cast as Alex Keaton on NBCs *Family Ties*, which ran seven seasons, won him three *Emmys* and made him a household name in the U.S. Other prominent roles include Marty McFly in the *Back to the Future* trilogy, *The Secret of My Success, Casualties of War* and *Doc Hollywood*, plus voiceovers.

73

Jamie Foxx (December 13, 1967-_____) American actor, singer, comedian, writer and producer
Birth Name — Eric Marion Bishop

2005, Navy, Public Domain

Foxx was born in Terrell, Texas. As a baby he was adopted and raised by his mother's adoptive parents in a segregated environment. His Baptist grandmother had a big influence on his life. He began playing piano at age five, and later was a pianist and choir leader at their church. In 2nd grade he was so adept at telling jokes that his teacher would reward the class by letting Jamie tell jokes. In high school he played football and had ambitions to play for the Dallas Cowboys. He got a scholarship to the U.S. International College where he studied classical music and composition.

He first started telling jokes publically at an open-mic night at a comedy club in 1989. He noticed that female performers were most often given first place on the billing so he changed his name in hopes that he would be taken for a girl and get put first on stage. He hasn't had that problem for many years now. The name Foxx was as a tribute to **Redd Foxx.**[69] In 1991 he joined the cast of *In Living Color*, which opened doors to his great career, including his own television show.

Redd Foxx (December 9, 1922 – October 11, 1991) American comedian and actor
Birth Name — John Elroy Sanford

1966 Publicity Photo, Public Domain

Foxx was born in St. Louis, Missouri. His father, Fred Sanford, an electrician and auto mechanic from Kentucky left his family when Redd was four years old, and he was raised by his half-Seminole Indian mother in Chicago on the South Side. His older brother, Fred G. Sanford, Jr. provided the name for his unforgettable character in *Sanford and Son*. On July 27, 1939, Redd preformed as member of the **Jump Swinging Six** on a local radio show called *Major Bowes Amateur Hour*.

Then in the '40s he was an associate of Malcolm Little, later known as **Malcolm X.** In his autobiography Malcolm called him "Chicago Red," saying that he was "the funniest dishwasher on this earth." After playing raunchy nightclubs beginning in the '50s, he signed a contract for comedy records. He picked up Malcolm's "Red," adding another d to match the surname, Foxx which he adopted from baseball star, **Jimmie Foxx,**[70] nicknamed Double X, who played for the Red Sox. He was best known for his *Sanford* role and his Party Records.

75

Anthony Franciosa (October 25, 1928 – January 19, 2006) American film, Television and stage actor
Birth Name — Anthony George Papaleo

1969 Publicity Photo, Public Domain

Born to Italian-American parents in New York City, he adopted his mother's maiden name as his stage name.[71] In 1948 he joined the Cherry Lane Theater Group Off Broadway at the same time as actress **Bea Arthur** (also featured), and within two years he was a member of the Actor's Studio. While striving for success as an actor, he worked odd jobs.

His first recognition was in the Broadway performance of *A Hatful of Rain*, which earned him a Tony. He reprised this role in the film rendition in 1957 for which he was nominated for an Oscar for Best Actor. This was followed by several other major film roles including *A Face in the Crowd* (1957) with **Andy Griffith** and **Patricia Neal**; *The Naked Maja* (1958), with **Ava Gardner**; *The Long Hot Summer* (1958), with **Paul Newman** and **Orson Welles**; and *Career* (1959) with **Dean Martin** and **Shirley MacLaine**, for which he won an Oscar for Best Actor, and several others.

76

Lady Gaga (March 28, 1986-_____) American metal/rock singer and songwriter
Birth Name—Stephanie Joanne Angelina Germanotta

2015 Tour, Flickr.com/photos, CC

Born in Manhattan, the elder of two daughters in a Catholic family, Stephanie attended the Covenant of the Sacred Heart School on the Upper East Side. She didn't feel like she fit in and was often made fun of, and in her own words, "felt like a freak." She started playing piano at age four, wrote her first piano ballad at 13, and started performing at open-mics at age 14. She was given lead roles in high school productions including Adelaide in *Girls and Dolls* and Philia in *A Funny Thing Happened on the Way to the Forum.* She even got a small television part in an episode of *The Sopranos* in 2001.

After high school she applied for early admission to a musical theater training conservatory at NYU's Tisch School of the Arts, where she lived in the dorm at age 17. She wrote essays and auditioned for and won a part in MTV's *Boiling Points.* Dropping out at 19 to focus on music, she met producer **Rob Fusari**, who compared her to **Queen** lead singer **Freddie Mercury**. He named her Lady Gaga after the Queen song *Radio Ga Ga.*[72] Her greatest work began in 2008 with release of *The Fame.*

Greta Garbo (18 September 1905 – 15 April 1990) Swedish-born silent film actress
Birth Name – Greta Lovisa Gustafsson

1935 MGM Photo, Public Domain

Born in Stockholm, Sweden, Garbo was the youngest child of a laborer and lived in a city slum. As a child she was a shy daydreamer who hated school, but an avid reader, and developed an interest in theater at a young age, dreaming of becoming an actress. In school she participated in amateur theater. After graduating at 13, she cared for her father when he became ill with Spanish flu and died at her age 14.

While working at a department store, she began modeling hats for their catalogues. In late 1920 the store's film director began casting her in commercials for women's clothing. In 1922 she caught the attention of director **Erik Arthur Petschler** who gave her a part in *Peter and the Tramp*, a short comedy film. For two years she attended acting school. In 1924 she was recruited for her first part in *The Saga of Gösta Berling*. Swedish director **Mauritz Stiller** coached her and convinced her to change her name to Garbo.[73] He took her to Hollywood and introduced her to **Louis B. Meyer**, president of MGM who was anxious to give her a Hollywood contract.

Judy Garland (June 10, 1922 – June 22, 1969) American singer, actress and vaudeville performer
Birth Name — Frances Ethel Gumm

1946 Publicity Photo, Public Domain

Born in Grand Rapids, Michigan, her parents were vaudevillians who ran a movie theater there. She began performing at age 2 ½ with her two older sisters, singing Jingle Bells. Amid rumors that her father was gay, they moved to Lancaster, California, where her father bought another theater. While she attended high school, her mother tried to get the girls into movies. After graduation, they all enrolled in a dance school run by Ethel Meglin, entering Meglin Kiddies' Dance Troup, debuting in 1929 in *The Big Revue. A Holiday in Storyland,* 1930, featured her first on-screen solo.

It is uncertain how she got her stage name of Garland. One story is that it was given by **George Jessel**, with whom they worked in Chicago, after **Carol Lombard**'s character, Lilly Garland in *Twentieth Century.*[74] Another is that they took it from film critic, **George Garland**. Judy's daughter, Lorna Luft, said that her mother chose it when Jessel said the girls looked like a garland of flowers. At any rate, they all became the Garland Sisters in 1934, and Frances took the name Judy right after that.

Elizabeth Garner (23 March 1892 – 12 November 1973) Scottish-born Dominican writer and politician
Birth Name — Elma Gordon-Cumming

Circa 1920 Photo, Public Domain

This colorful author was born in Scotland as the eldest of five children **of Sir William Gordon-Cumming**, a Scottish Lt-Col., adventurer, socialite, and a friend of **Edward, Prince of Wales** (later **King Edward II**). Her father's reputation having been ruined before her birth in what was known as the *Royal Baccarat Scandal*; to compensate through marriage to legitimatize her name, she married **Captain Maurice Antony Crutchley Gibbs** in 1912 and moved to Australia.

But nine years later she fell in love with another English businessman, **Lennox Pelham Napier**, and divorced Gibbs, loosing custody of their two children. In 1924 she married Napier and had two more children.

They visited the Caribbean in 1931 and moved the following year to the Dominican coast. She took her mother's maiden name, changing her first name to Elizabeth[75] and wrote two novels set in Dominica in the 1930s and three memoirs on different parts of her life in different countries, the last published posthumously. Her husband died in 1940.

James Garner (April 7, 1928- July 19, 2014) American actor, voice artist, and comedian
Birth Name — James Scott Bumgarner

1959 (*Maverick*), Public Domain

After a friend convinced him while he was in high school in 1954 to take a non-speaking role in the Broadway production of *The Caine Mutiny Court-Martial*, he studied **Henry Fonda**'s acting techniques every night, which had a profound influence on his career. Soon he was doing television commercials and small television spots. In 1957 he got a supporting role in an episode of the TV anthology *Conflict* titled *Man from 1997*. The show's producer, **Roy Higgins**, then cast Bumgarner for the leading role in *Maverick* based on his comedic facial expressions in that show.

He changed his name to James Garner when the studio credited him that way without permission.[76] He legally changed it on the birth of his first child. In a career which has spanned over five decades, Garner has appeared in numerous other television shows and has played in more than 50 motion pictures, receiving an Oscar for his performance in *Murphy's Romance* (1985).

Tracey Gold (May 16, 1969) American actress and former child star
Birth Name — Tracey Claire Fisher

Tracey Gold Official Website, fair use

Born in New York City to advertising executive, Bonny Fisher, she and younger sister, actress **Missy Gold**, both changed their names after being adopted by Harry Goldstein, who married their mother when Tracey was in preschool. They used a shortened form to avoid ethnic stereotyping.[77] They have three younger half-sisters, two of which are actors, who also use the name Gold.

Tracy began acting at age four, after appearing on a Pepsi Cola print ad, first appearing in two television series which were soon cancelled: *Shirley*, with **Shirley Jones** (1979), and *Goodnight Beantown* starring **Bill Bixby** (1983). In the pilot she was cast in *Gimme a Break*, but was replaced by **Lara Jean Miller** in the series. Her big break came in the role for which she is best known, that of Carol in *Growing Pains* which ran from 1985 till 1992.

Afterward she starred in several television movies. She is also widely known for her battle with anorexia nervosa which almost killed her.

Whoopi Goldberg (November 15, 1955-_____) American comedienne, actress, political activist, writer and television host
Birth Name — Caryn Elaine Johnson

2008 Bob Marley Competition,
David Sharkbone, Creative Commons Attribution- Share Alike

Obviously simplicity was not the determining factor here. The story was told that her first name was chosen from the fact that her family passed a lot of gas...(she *is* a comedian). Goldberg explained it this way, "If you get a little gassy, you've got to let it go. So people used to say to me, 'you're like a whoopee cushion.' And that's where the name came from."[78]

He mother reportedly told her she should choose a Jewish last name because it would help her career if people thought she was Jewish! What a switch from the norm.

Although she had already made her debut in 1982, her real breakthrough was the role of Cecile in *The Color Purple* (1985) with Oprah Winfrey and Danny Glover. For this she was nominated for an Oscar. Then her role as a psychic in *Ghost* (1990) won her an Oscar for Best Supporting Actress. She is one of few with an Oscar, a Grammy and a Tony to her credit.

83

Cary Grant (January 18, 1904 – November 29, 1986) English stage and Hollywood film actor
Birth Name — Archibald Alexander Leach

1941 RKO; *Suspicion*, Public Domain

Born in Horfield, Bristol, UK, he was the only surviving child of a pants presser father and had an unhappy childhood. Due to the death of a previous child, his mother suffered from clinical depression, and his father put her in a mental institution when Archie was nine, telling him that she was on a long holiday. He later was told that she had died, and his father remarried and had a new family without him. Only at his age 32 did his father, near his death, confess that she was still living.

Expelled from grammar school at age 12, Leach joined the **Bob Pender Stage Troupe** and traveled to the United States. At age 16 he was processed at Ellis Island on July 28, 1920. When his troupe returned to England he stayed in the U.S. to continue his stage career, touring in a vaudeville act as Parker, Rand and Leach.

Still using his birth name he performed in several plays in St. Louis in 1931. He became a U.S. citizen in 1942, changing his name to Cary Grant,[79] starring in many films, and was named second *Greatest Male Star of All Time* by the American Film Institute.

Macy Gray (September 6, 1967-_____) American R&B and soul singer, songwriter, musician, record producer and actress
Birth Name — Natalie Renee McIntyre

Macy Gray Performs in Memphis, 2011, Creative Commons Attribution- S/A

Born in Canton, Ohio, the city in which I first entered school, her mother was a math teacher and her father an insurance broker who left them when she was small. Her mother later remarried. She studied scriptwriting at the University of Southern California where she wrote songs for a friend which were to be demoed by another singer. When the selected vocalist was a no show at the session, Grey sang them herself.

While working as a cashier in Beverly Hills she met producer **Joe Solo** with whom she collaborated to compose a group of songs which were recorded at Solo's studio. This demo gave her the in to sing at jazz cafés in Los Angeles. That's when she decided to change her name. As a kid she had fallen off her bike at a mailbox of a man named Macy Gray.[80]

She got married and pregnant, but after three children she divorced. She was first signed to Atlantic Records, then Epic Records in 1998. Her debut album in 1999, *On How Life Is,* became a worldwide hit, selling seven million copies. In 2001 she won a Grammy for Best Female Pop Vocal performance for *I Try*, which was nominated for Song of the Year.

Lorne Greene (February 12, 1915 – September 11, 1987) Canadian actor and musician
Birth Name – Lyon Hiram Green

1969 Photo, Public Domain

Born in Ottawa, Ontario, Canada to Russian Jewish immigrants, he was called "Chaim" by his mother and "Hyman" on his report cards, so this future star was accustomed to being called by names other than his own from his youth. In his daughter Linda Greene Bennett's 2004 book, *My Father's Voice: The Biography of Lorne Greene*, she stated that it was not known when he started using Lorne or added the e to Green.[81]

He was a drama teacher at a summer camp in Algonquin Park, Ontario, where his talents were developed. He started acting while a student at Queen's University in Kingston, where he broadcast over campus radio station CFRC.

After graduating he went to work for CBC, becoming the principle news reader for the national broadcast, and was nicknamed "The Voice of Canada." He also narrated documentary films. In 1957 he played the prosecutor in *Peyton Place*. In 1959 he landed the role of Ben Cartwright on NBC's color blockbuster *Bonanza*, running 14 years.

Ann Harding (August 7, 1902 – September 1, 1981) American theater, motion picture and television actress
Birth Name — Dorothy Walton Gatley

1930 Publicity Photo, Public Domain

The daughter of a military officer, Harding was born in Fort Sam Houston, San Antonio, Texas, and grew up in Orange, New Jersey. After attending Bryn Mawr College outside Pittsburg, she began working as a script reader and made her Broadway debut in 1921, where she first used the pseudonym, Ann Harding,[82] which she had concocted at the age of ten.

Just eight years later she made her film debut in *Paris Bound* opposite **Fredric March**. In 1931 she was nominated for an Oscar for *Holiday* (1930) with **Edward Everett Horton**. Other outstanding performances include *Animal Kingdom* (1932), with **Leslie Howard**, *Westward Passage* (1932) with **Laurence Olivier** and *The Man in the Grey Flannel Suit* (1956), again with March. She had taken a break, however, when she married famed conductor and score writer, **Werner Janssen**, in 1937. Janssen is the grandfather of one of my friends on social media (see front photo).

She was called *Cinema's Gallant Lady* in a 2010 biography for the roles which she played so well.

Hawkshaw Hawkins (December 22, 1921 – March 5, 1963) American country music singer
Birth Name—Harold Franklin Hawkins

Grand Ole Opry Archives, Public Domain

Born in Huntington, West Virginia, Hawkins got his nickname as a youngster after helping a neighbor track down two missing fishing rods. The neighbor dubbed him "Hawkshaw" after the title character in a comic strip titled, *Hawkshaw the Detective*.[83]

He used his first guitar, gotten in trade for rabbits which he had trapped, to perform on WCMI-AM radio in Ashland, Kentucky. At just 16, he won a talent contest and a job on WSAZ-AM in Huntington, West Virginia.

At age 19 he married his 16 year old girlfriend and enlisted in the Army, serving as an engineer near Paris, Texas where he entertained at local clubs. During World War II, as a staff sergeant he was stationed in France and fought in the Battle of the Bulge winning four battle stars. After the war he signed with King Records and had top ten records right away. Hawkins was killed in the same plane crash that took the lives of **Patsy Cline** and **Cowboy Copas** (also featured).

Audrey Hepburn (May 4, 1929-January 20, 1993) British actress and humanitarian
Birth Name — Audrey Kathleen Ruston

1954 Portrait by *Bud Fraker*,
Public Domain

Born in Brussels, Belgium, Audrey's father, Joseph, was a British subject of Austrian descent born in Úžice, Bohemia. His father had once been an honorary consul in the British West Indies and erroneously believed himself to be descended from **James Hepburn**, the 3rd husband of **Mary, Queen of Scots,** so Joseph changed their name to Hepburn-Ruston.[84]

Audrey's mother, Baroness Ella van Heemstra, was truly a Dutch aristocrat, daughter of **Baron Aarnoud van Heemstra,** once governor of Dutch Suriname. Her parents married in Dutch Colonial Batavia in 1926 then moved to Belgium. Her mother found her father in bed with the children's nanny, leading to their divorce.

During the war she took the pseudonym Edda van Heemstra because her name was too English during German Occupation. After the war she moved to Amsterdam, studied ballet, and appeared in her first film in 1948. For the stage she kept the name Hepburn dropping Ruston. She was the first actress to win an Oscar for the lead in *Roman Holiday*.

O. Henry (September 11, 1862- June 6, 1911) American writer
Birth Name—William Sidney Porter

1909 Portrait by *W. Vanderweyde*

Porter was born in Goldsboro, North Carolina. His mother died when he was three. As a child he read a lot. His aunt was his teacher and he graduated at age 13, enrolling in high school. She tutored him for two more years then he began work at his uncle's drug store. By 19 he was a licensed pharmacist. The next year, he moved to Texas for his health and worked on a ranch. Improved, he moved to Austin in 1884 working as a part-time journalist. He married Athol Estes, a sickly girl from a wealthy family who encouraged him to write.

While a draftsman then a bank teller he submitted articles. He was hired by a weekly, *The Rolling Stone,* then wrote for the *Houston Post*. Accused of embezzlement, he fled to Honduras, where he wrote *Cabbages and Kings*. Athol became very ill in Austin, so he returned and surrendered. She died and he was sentenced to five years, serving three. He was a pharmacist in prison and wrote under various pen names, but became best known as O. Henry, first used on *Whistling Dick's Christmas Stocking* in the December, 1899 issue of *McClure's Magazine*. The name may have come from a prison guard.[85]

Charlton Heston (October 4, 1923 – April 5, 2008) American actor and political activist
Birth Name — John Charles Carter

1953 Publicity Photo, Public Domain

Carter was born in rural Illinois, the son of a sawmill operator and construction-worker father. While very young, his family moved to a rural area near St. Helen, Michigan where he spent time hunting and fishing as a youth, and acting out characters from books he read. At his age 10, his parents divorced and his mother married Chester Heston. The family then moved back to the suburbs of Chicago, Illinois. There in high school he enrolled in New Trier's drama program, playing in a silent 16mm film adaptation of **Henrik Ibsen's** play, *Peer Grant,* produced by **David Bradley**. At that time he took his stage name from his mother's maiden name, Charleston and his stepfather's surname.[86] He earned a drama scholarship to Northwestern University where one of his teachers was **Alvina Krause**. Later he worked with Bradley again to produce the first film version *of Julius Caesar* in which he played Mark Antony. After marrying classmate Lydia Marie Clark, he enlisted in the Army Air Forces and served two years. After the couple managed a playhouse in Asheville, North Carolina, they moved to New York where he starred on Broadway. His real fame came in movies, starring in 100 films over six decades. He is best remembered for his immortal role as Moses in **Cecil B. DeMille's** classic epic, *The Ten Commandments* (1956).

91

Hulk Hogan (August 11, 1953-_____) American professional wrestler, actor, TV personality, entrepreneur and musician
Birth Name — Terry Jean Bollea

1984 Publicity Photo, Fair use

Born in Augusta, Georgia, Hogan is the son of a construction foreman and a dance instructor. As a small child the family moved to Port Tampa, Florida. As a youth he wanted to play professional baseball but an injury ended that. At 16 he was attracted to professional wrestling and was inspired by "Superstar" Billy Graham, wanting to match his "inhuman" look. He also played fretless bass guitar.

Dropping out of the University of South Florida, he and two friends started a band called **Ruckus** in 1976. He worked out at a local gym, and wrestlers frequented bars where his band played, including **Jack** and **Gerald Brisco**. Impressed by Hogan's physique, they asked championship trainer **Hiro Matsuda** to consider him for training. In spite of setbacks, he quit the band and began telling people that he was going to be a wrestler. He was accepted in mid-1977. Later, after being on TV with **Lou Ferrigno**, who played *The Incredible Hulk*, he began performing as Terry "The Hulk" Boulder,[87] later changing it to Hulk Hogan. He was very popular in the '80s and '90s.

Billie Holiday (April 7, 1915 – July 17, 1959) American jazz singer and songwriter
Birth Name — Eleanora Fagan

1930s Publicity Photo, Public Domain

Born in Philadelphia, Pennsylvania to unwed parents, her father was likely Clarence Holiday, but she was given her mother, "Sadie's" surname name at birth. Soon, Holiday left to become a jazz guitarist. Rejected by her parents, Sadie went to live with her married half-sister, Eva. Eleanora was often brought before juvenile authorities. Placed in a Catholic reform school, she was paroled to her mother, who worked her long hours in a café. By age 11 she dropped out of school. One day her mother found a neighbor trying to rape her, and had him arrested. Eleanora was then sent back to the reform school. After her release at not quite 12 she got a job running errands at a brothel, and was listening to **Louis Armstrong** and **Bessie Smith** records. She joined her mother in Harlem working as a prostitute. The brothel was raided and both were sent to prison. She was released at 14. She started singing, taking her stage name from **Billie Dove**, an actress she admired, [88] and her probable father. First signed by **John Hammond** to Brunswick Records, and nicknamed "Lady Day," she went on to become one of the most influential jazz and blues singers of her time.

Buddy Holly (September 7, 1936 – February 3, 1959) American musician and singer-songwriter

Birth Name — Charles Hardin Holley

C 1957 Record Promotion Photo,
Public Domain

This famed pioneer of rock-and-roll was born in Texas, the fourth child of Baptist parents. He was nicknamed "Buddy" by his family. The Holleys had a great interest in music, and all could play except Buddy, performing in local talent shows.

At 11 Buddy took piano lessons, but switched to guitar, buying one at a pawn shop, which his brother, Travis, taught him to play. Influenced by stars like the **Louvin Brothers**, he teamed up with friend, Jack Neal, and won a local television contest. After high school he pursued music, seeing **Elvis Presley** live, and later opening for him. Putting a band together, he switched to rock-and-roll. In October, 1955, **Paul Cohen** signed them to Decca Records, and misspelled his last name. From then on, he was Buddy Holly.[89] After other names, his band became the Crickets, and they rose to great success. He was killed with two other stars when their plane went down "The Day the Music Died."

Bob Hope (May 29, 1903 – July 27, 2003) English comedian, vaudevillian, actor, singer, dancer, athlete, and author
Birth Name — Leslie Townes Hope

1978, Public Domain

Hope was the first of seven sons of a stone mason father and light opera singer mother. He was born in Eltham, London. In 1908 the family immigrated to the U.S. and from age 12, he earned money from busking, singing, dancing and doing comedy in Ohio. He entered numerous amateur talent contests as Leslie Hope, winning in 1915 for his impersonation of **Charlie Chaplin**. After briefly attending Boys Industrial School in Cleveland and working as an assistant lineman, he decided on a show business career, and he and his girlfriend signed up for dance classes and got a three day gig at a club. He formed a partnership with a friend and silent film comedian, **Fatty Arbuckle** saw them perform in 1925 and got them work with a touring troupe. Within a year Hope had formed an act which included conjoined twins, the **Hilton Sisters,** and played on vaudeville. In 1929, he changed his name to Bob, reportedly after racecar driver **Bob Burman**.[90] He began on radio in 1934 and TV in the 1950s. He started USO shows in 1941, and made over 70 films and shorts, including *Road* movies with **Bing Crosby**.

Harry Houdini (March 24, 1874 – October 31, 1926) Hungarian
American Illusionist and escape artist
Birth Name — Erick Weiss

1899 Photo, *McManus-Young Collection*, PD

Born in Budapest, Austria-Hungary, he was one of seven children of a
Jewish Rabbi. He arrived in the United States with his pregnant mother
and four brothers on July 3, 1878. The family changed the spelling of
their name to the German rendition, Weiss, and Erick's name was
changed to Ehrich, but his friends called him either Ehrie or "Harry."
The father came later and they moved to Wisconsin where he served a
Zion Reform Jewish congregation. After becoming an American citizen,
his father first took Ehrich and moved to New York City, later being
joined by the rest of the family. Ehrich went to work as a trapeze artist at
age nine as Enrich, the Prince of the Air. After also becoming a champion
runner, he became a magician, changing his name to Harry Houdini in
homage to American magician, **Harry Keller** (though already answering
to "Harry") and French magician **Jean Eugène Robert-Houdin.**[91] Little
did anyone know that his fame would far outlive either of them, becoming the most accomplished escape artist of all time.

Rock Hudson (November 17, 1925 – October 2, 1985) American actor
Birth Name – Leroy Harold Scherer, Jr.

1955 Publicity Photo, Public Domain

Born in Winnetka, Illinois, Hudson was the only child of a telephone operator mother and an auto mechanic father who abandoned them during the Great Depression. His mother remarried Wally Fitzgerald who adopted him and changed his name to Fitzgerald. He was a shy boy, but sang in his school's glee club and caddied at the golf course as a youth. After serving as a naval aircraft mechanic during World War II, he moved to Los Angeles to pursue acting, but was denied admission to the University of Southern California's drama program because of poor grades. In 1947 he sent a picture of himself to talent scout **Henry Wilson**, who changed his name to Rock Hudson.[92] His debut was with Warner Brothers in *Fighter Squadron* (1948). Soon he was being featured in film magazines and heavily promoted for his acting, singing, dancing and fencing. This led to many leading roles like *Magnificent Obsession* with **Jane Wyman** (1954) and *Giant* (1956), for which both he and co-star **James Dean** were nominated for Best Actor Oscars. He co-starred with **Doris Day** in 3 romantic comedies in the '60s. He died of AIDS in 1985.

Engelbert Humperdinck (May 2, 1936-_____) Indian-born, German decent British pop singer
Birth Name – Arnold George Dorsey

2009 Los Vegas,
Creative Commons Attribution- Share Alike

In the early 1950s Arnold was a saxophone player and impressionist in the UK. Because of his excellent imitation of **Jerry Lewis** early in his career, friends began calling him Gerry Dorsey, a name he went by on stage for almost ten years. Though he had recorded earlier, with little success, in 1965, he teamed up with **Gordon Mills**, a former friend who was now a music impresario and was managing **Tom Jones**. Because he was aware of Dorsey's struggles in the industry, Mills suggested he change his name to that of famed nineteenth century German opera composer, **Engelbert Humperdinck**,[93] to get the attention of the industry and create a new start. He adopted the name professionally but not legally, and Mills negotiated him a new contract with Decca Records. His success came in 1966. In Germany he only uses Engelbert because the family of the composer will not allow him to use their family name there.

Betty Hutton (February 26, 1921 – March 11, 2007) American stage, film and television actress, comedian and singer
Birth Name – Elizabeth June Thornburg

1944 Publicity Photo, Public Domain

She was the daughter of a railroad foreman and alcoholic mother, and was born in Battle Creek, Michigan. When she was very young her father abandoned her and her mother and sister for another woman and later committed suicide. The three started singing when she was three years old. Her mother, Mabel, later took the surname Hutton,[94] giving it to her daughters as well, and Betty was short for Elizabeth. Her mother later acted as Sissy Jones. Betty sang in bands as a teen but was rejected in New York for Broadway. A few years later **Vincent Lopez**, an orchestra leader, scouted her and got her started. In 1939 she played in musical shorts for Warner Brothers, and won a supporting role in *Panama Hattie* on Broadway starring **Ethel Merman** who demanded on opening night that Hutton's musical numbers be cut from the show. She also got into *Two for the Show* that year. In 1942 director **Buddy DeSylva** had begun producing for Paramount Pictures and signed Hutton for *The Fleet's In*. She was an instant hit, making 19 films between 1942 and '52 including *The Perils of Pauline, Let's Dance* and *Annie Get your Gun*.

Ice Cube (June 5, 1969-_____) American rapper, record producer, actor, and filmmaker
Birth Name — O'Shea Jackson, Sr.

2014 Chicago Publicity *Adam Bielawski*, Creative Commons Attribution- Share Alike

Born in Los Angeles, California, the son of a hospital clerk mother and UCLA groundskeeper father, he underwent great trauma at age 12 when his half-sister was murdered by her boyfriend. He developed an interest in hip hop music in his early teens and began writing raps in high school keyboard class. With friend **Sir Jinx** he formed the **C.I.A.** and began performing at parties hosted by **Dr. Dre** and soon began recording as a member of **World Class Wreckin' Crew**. Soon he and **Dr. Dre** were co-writing and recorded *She's a Stag* on Epic Records in 1986. In the fall of 1987 he enrolled in Phoenix Institute of Technology studying architectural drafting, but that same year he recorded *My Posse* as **C.I.A.**

Ice Cube got his stage name from his older brother who thought he was "too cool" and started calling him that as a young boy.[95] His lyrics are often political as well as violent and aggressive, causing controversy.

Vanilla Ice (October 31, 1967-_____) American rapper, actor, and television host
Birth Name: Robert Matthew Van Winkle

2007, *Dave Kleinschmidt* (cropped), Creative Commons Attribution- Share Alike

Born in Dallas, Texas, Robert has never known his biological father, and took the family name of his mother's husband at birth. At his age 4, his mother divorced, and he grew up between Dallas and Miami, where his mother's new husband worked at an auto dealership. A lover of poetry by his own admission, hip hop had an influence on him from his early childhood. As an early teen he practiced break-dancing and his friends nicknamed him 'Vanilla,' as he was the only group member that was not African American. Though not fond of the name, it stuck, and later he was called MC Vanilla. But when he joined a break-dancing group he became Vanilla Ice because one of his moves was called 'The Ice.'[96]

He then moved back to Texas and attended high school, because his stepfather got a better job there. His debut album, *Hooked*, was released in 1989, and his 1990 single, *Ice Ice Baby*, was his first top-ten single.

Ice-T (February 16, 1958-_____) American rapper, singer and actor

Birth Name — Tracy Lauren Marrow

1989 *Raymond Boyd/Michael Ochs Archives*, Fair use

Millions know him as "Fin" on NBC's popular *Law and Order, SVU*, but long before he was there he became famous for his rap music, first signing at Sire Records in 1987, and soon founding his own label, Rhyme Syndicate based on the title of his first album, *Rhyme Pays*. In spite of his firm stance on not partaking in alcohol, tobacco and drugs, in his autobiographical book, *Cold as Ice*, Morrow says he had a great interest in heavy metal music in high school in LA, many of his friends were gang members, and he became associated with the Crips. He had a fascination with the novels of **Iceberg Slim**, and would quote from them to his friends who said to him, "Yo, kick some more of that by Ice, T." This gave him the idea of using the moniker, Ice-T later.[97] He wrote and sung Crip Rhymes long before hip hop appeared on the scene, making him a pioneer in this genre. During his four-year stint in the Army, hip hop was becoming popular, and he was inspired by **Sugar Hill Gang**. After his discharge, he became a DJ and performed at parties, which gave him the incentive to begin a rapping career as Ice-T.

Billy Idol (November 30, 1955-_____) English rock musician, singer and actor
Birth Name—William Michael Broad

2012 Peace & Love Fest, *Possan,*
Creative Commons Attribution- Share Alike

Born in Stanmore, Middlesex, England, his stage name was inspired by a high school teacher's description of him as being "Idol."[98]

At Billy's age two, his family moved to Long Island, New York. A sister, Jane, was born before they returned to England four years later. After moving to Bromley in Southeast London, he attended Ravensbourne School for Boys, then Worthing High School for boys in West Sussex. From there he went to Sussex University, leaving after only one year to join the Bromley Contingent of Sex Pistols Fans, a gang who followed the band when in town. In 1977 he joined **Chelsea**, an English punk rock band, as a guitarist, soon leaving with **Tony James** to found **Generation X**, in which Idol was lead singer. They were one of the first punk rock bands to appear on BBC TV's Top of the Pops, and signed with Chrystalis Records releasing three albums. Idol went on to a major solo career.

David Janssen (March 27, 1931 – February 13, 1980) American film and television actor
Birth Name – David Harold Meyer

1963 *Fugitive* **Photo,** Public Domain

Born in Naponee, Franklin County, Nebraska, he was the son of a banker and was of Irish and Jewish descent. After his parents' divorce, at his age five, he moved with his mother to Los Angeles, California, where she married Eugene Janssen. David used his stepfather's name when he entered show business as a child.[99]

He got his first film part at age thirteen. He attended high school and by the age of 25 he had appeared in twenty films and served two years in the U.S. Army. During his stint in the service he became friends with **Martin Milner** and **Clint Eastwood** while stationed at Fort Ord, California. Janssen had appeared in several TV series before landing the role for which he is best known, Dr. Richard Kimble in United Artists production, *The Fugitive* (1963-1967), aired on CBS. The show was rated number 36 on *TV Guide*'s **50 Greatest TV Shows of All Time**.

Elton John (March 25, 1947-_____) English pop-rock singer, hit songwriter, composer, record producer and actor
Birth Name — Reginald Kenneth Dwight

2011, Tribeca Film Fest,
David Shankbone, Creative Commons Attribution- Share Alike

Born in Pinner, Middlesex, he was raised in a council house. After his parents married at his age six, they moved to a semi-detached house nearby, but divorced at his age 14. He played music from age 3, studying it in school. Both parents were musically inclined, and when his mother remarried, his stepfather was supportive, though his military father tried to steer him to a conventional career. His mother's purchase of records by **Elvis Presley** and **Bill Haley and His Comets** hooked him on rock and roll. By age 15 he was playing piano at a local pub, and soon started a band called Bluesology, and in about three years they were backing touring American soul and R&B groups like the **Isley Brothers** and **Patty LaBelle and the Bluebelles**. In 1966 they became **Long John Baldry's** supporting band playing at the Marquee Club. Elton changed his name in honor of two of his idols: **Elton Dean** and **Long John Baldry**.[100] He has received six Grammys and sold more than 300 million records.

Grandpa Jones (October 20, 1913 – February 19, 1998), American banjo player, country and gospel music singer, comedian and television star
Birth Name – Louis Marshall Jones

PBS, Public Domain

Born in rural Henderson County, Kentucky, Jones spent his teen years in Akron, Ohio, where he began singing country music on AM radio station WJW. In 1931 he joined the Pine Ridge String Band which accompanied **Lum and Abner**, a popular duo of the day. By 1935 he was at WBZ in Boston, where he met musician **Bradley Kincaid**, who gave him the moniker 'Grandpa Jones' because of his grumpiness in their early morning broadcasts at the ripe old age of 21. He thought the name fit and adapted makeup to suit the part.[101]

During the '30s his career took him to radio stations from West Virginia to Connecticut and Ohio, and got him involved with other popular country entertainers of the day, and he and **Merle Travis**, under the name the **Shepherd Brothers**, became the first to record on the new King Label. But his later appearances at the *Grand Ole Opry* and his presence on *Hee-Haw*, the longest running show of its type, made him immortal.

Jennifer Jones (March 2, 1919-December 17, 2009) American Academy Award winning film actress
Birth Name: Phyllis Lee Isley

1955 Movie Photo, Public Domain

Born in Tulsa, Oklahoma, she was raised Roman Catholic. Her parents toured the Midwest in a traveling tent show that they owned and operated. She first attended a junior college, then Northwestern University in Illinois, transferring to the American Academy of Dramatic Arts in New York City in 1938. There she met and married fellow acting student **Robert Walker**. They went to Tulsa for a 13-week radio program before moving to Hollywood. She landed two small roles, but when she failed a screen test for Paramount Pictures the couple returned to New York City. While Walker found radio work, she modeled hats. Auditions were being held for **Rose Franken's** hit play, *Claudia*, and she went. After what she felt was a bad reading, she left in tears. **David O. Selznick**, however, overheard her audition and was impressed and asked his secretary to call her back, signing her to a 7 year contract. Here she was given the name Jennifer Jones.[102] **Henry King** chose her for the lead in *Song of Burnadette,* winning the Oscar, and the rest is history!

Wynonna Judd (May 30, 1964-_____) American country music singer

Birth Name — Christina Claire Ciminella

2006, Open Arms Performance Photo, Public Domain

Born in Ashland Kentucky, she was given the surname Ciminella after her step-father. Her biological father, Charles Jordan, had abandoned her mother. While her younger half-sister, actress **Ashley Judd**, and she were young, their mother moved them to Los Angeles, divorcing Ciminella in 1972. By 1976 Wynonna and **Naomi** were back in Kentucky. There Wynonna received a guitar for Christmas, inspired by the country music her mother listened to. In 1979, the two moved to Nashville in pursuit of a musical career. In 1983 RCA Records signed them as **The Judds** (Naomi's maiden name).[103] Wynonna got her new moniker from the lyrics to the old swing song *Route 66 — Flagstaff, Arizona/Don't forget Wynona.*[104] By 1991 they had released 6 albums and had won 5 Grammys as Best Country Duo and eight CMA awards. Naomi was diagnosed with Hepatitis C in 1991, and Wynona announced that she would begin a solo career, which she did in 1992 with the release of *New Day Dawning.*

Diane Keaton (January 5, 1946-_____) American film actress
Birth Name — Diane Hall

2011, *Firroz Zahedi-* Creative Commons Attribution- Share Alike, OTRS

Diane was born in Los Angeles, California to a real estate broker and civil engineer father and armature photographer homemaker mother, who won the *Mrs. Los Angeles* pageant for homemakers. According to Keaton, the theatricality of this event inspired her to want to become an actress. She was also inspired by **Katherine Hepburn**'s portrayals of strong, independent women. While still in high school at Santa Anna she participated in singing and acting clubs and starred as Blanche DuBois in a school production of *A Streetcar Named Desire*. While at Santa Anna College and West Coast College she was an acting student, but dropped out after a year at West Coast to pursue acting in Manhattan, where she studied at Neighborhood Playhouse.

She changed her name to her mother's maiden name because there was already a Diane Hall listed in the Actors' Guild.[105] Coincidentally, she wound up starring in the motion picture as Annie Hall in 1977.

Michael Keaton (September 5, 1951-_____) American actor, producer, director and comedian
Birth Name — Michael Douglas

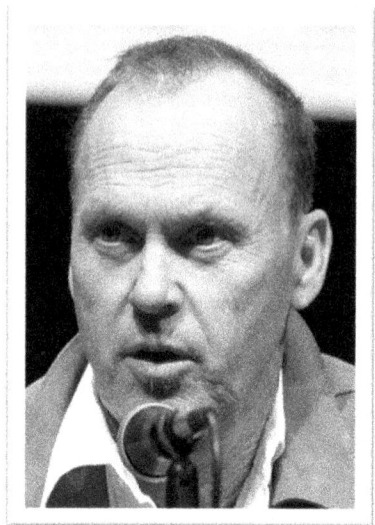

2013, San Diego, *Gage Skidmore*, Creative Commons Attribution- Share Alike

Born in Alleghany County, Pennsylvania, to a civil engineer and surveyor father and homemaker mother, he was raised Roman Catholic. After high school, he studied speech for two years at Kent State before dropping out and moving to Pittsburgh.

After being unsuccessful as a stand-up comic, he worked as a TV cameraman for public television station WQED. He first appeared on TV in *Where Is My Heart* and on *Mr. Rogers Neighborhood* as one of the **Flying Zookeeni Brothers**. He also served as full-time production assistant on that show. In 2004, following **Fred Rogers'** death, Keaton hosted a PBS memorial tribute show for him. He then went to Hollywood. Since his birth name was already being used, he was forced to choose another name. He settled on Keaton because of his affinity for the physical comedy of **Buster Keaton**.[106]

Alicia Keys (January 5, 1981-_____) American singer, songwriter and producer
Birth Name: Alicia Augello Cook

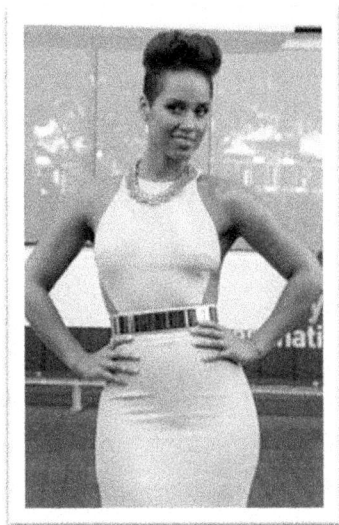

2013 Aria Awards, Sydney, Australia,
Eva Rinaldi, Creative Commons Attribution- Share Alike

Born in Hell's Kitchen, Manhattan, NYC, she is the only child of a paralegal, part-time actress mother and a flight attendant father. Her father is African American and her mother is Italian and English-Scottish. Her parents separated when she was two, and she was reared by her mother in Manhattan. Taking music and dance classes as a child, Keys studied classical piano from age seven, enrolling in Professional Performing Arts at age twelve, where she majored in choir and began writing songs at age 14. She graduated at age 16 as valedictorian. She met manager **Jeff Robinson** in 1994 who introduced her to Arista Records the next year. **Peter Edge** was extremely impressed with her talent and helped Robinson develop a showcase and demo material. She signed to Columbia, then Arista, but her Grammy-winning debut was by J Records. First having chosen Alicia Wild as a stage name, her manager suggested Keys because of a dream he had.[107]

Larry King (November 19. **1933-**_____) American television and radio host, voice artist and comedian
Birth Name — Lawrence Harvey Zeigler

2012 at Bill Myer Ceremony, *Angela George*, Creative Commons Attribution OTRS

Born in New York in the 1930s to Orthodox Jewish parents from Europe, King's father died of a heart attack at age 46 and his mother had to go on welfare. This greatly affected Larry, who went to work after high school to help support his mother, never attending college. He had an early desire to go into radio, and met a CBS staff announcer who suggested he move to Florida where there was a shortage of announcers. He went to Miami and got his first job at radio station WAHR (now WBMH) cleaning up and doing odd jobs. When one of their announcers quit, they put him on the air on May 1, 1957 and paid him $55.00 a week. The manager asked him to select a new surname to use on-air because he felt that Zeigler sounded too ethnic and difficult. Larry chose the name King which he got from an ad in *The Miami Herald* for King's Wholesale Liquor, minutes before air.[108] Within two years, he legally changed his name. His nighttime network TV talk shows won him many awards.

Ben Kingsley, Sir (August 31, 1933-_____) Award-winning
English-Indian actor best known for the role *Gandhi*
Birth Name — Krishna Pandit Bhanji

2012 Sundance Film Fest, *JP Evans*, Pub Dom

Born in Snainton, North Riding, Yorkshire, he was the son of a British
actress and model and an Indian doctor, who was actually born in
Kenya. His paternal grandfather was an extremely successful spice
trader who had moved to Zanzibar, where his father lived until moving
to England at the age of 14. His maternal grandfather was believed to be
of Russian or German Jewish background. He grew up near Manchester
where he was a classmate of **Robert Powell**, later to also become a well
known film star.

Having an Indian father, in the 1970s, actor Kingsley changed his name
fearing that a foreign name would hamper his career. He took his stage
name from his father's nickname of 'Benji' at Dulwich College and his
grandfather's nickname, 'King Cloves.'[109] He studied at the University of
Salford and Pendleton College, which later became the home of Ben
Kingsley Theater. His stage debut was upon graduation at age 23.

Patti LaBelle (May 24, 1944-_____) American singer and actor
Birth Name – Patricia Louise Holte-Edwards

1975, LaBelle
(center) with Blue Belles, Public Domain

Born in Philadelphia, Pennsylvania, Patti's father was a railroad worker and lounge singer, and her mother a homemaker. When she was 12, her parents divorced and her mother raised her and her three sisters as a single mother.

She was shy but had a gifted voice, singing in the choir at their Baptist church by age 10 and doing solos by 12. Known then as Patsy, she listened to gospel, jazz and R&B growing up. In 1958 she formed **The Ordettes** with three other friends. The next year, **Cindy Birdsong** left the group to join **Diana Ross and the Supremes**. Though upset, The Ordettes were still being noticed, and ran into Newtown Records president **Harold Robinson**, who auditioned them but thought "Patsy" was too plain and dark to lead a group, but signed them as the **Blue Belles**. Their first song made top twenty. Robinson was later sued over the group's name, and Patsy was given her new name, Patti LaBelle.[110]

Michael Landon (October 31, 1936 – July 1, 1991) American actor, writer, director and producer
Birth Name — Eugene Maurice Orowitz

1960s Publicity Photo, Public Domain

Born in Forest Hills, Queens, New York, his father was an actor and movie theater manager, and his mother a dancer and comedian. His father was Jewish and his mother was from an Irish Catholic family. At Eugene's age four they moved to Collingswood, New Jersey, a Philadelphia suburb. They attended a Conservative synagogue where he celebrated his Bar Mitzvah, then moved to Haddon Heights (now Cherry Hill), a neighborhood which did not allow Jews until after World War II. During childhood stress overwhelmed him about his mother's suicide attempts, causing a battle with bedwetting. He was an excellent javelin thrower and won an athletic scholarship to USC. These events inspired a television movie called *The Loneliest Runner* in 1976.

His first starring appearance was in the TV series *Telephone Time* which soon led to *I Was a Teenage Werewolf*. He chose his stage surname from a phone book listing.[111] He became a hit as Little Joe on NBC's *Bonanza* ('59-"73), then produced and starred in *Little House on the Prairie* ('74-'82).

115

Ralph Lauren (October 13, 1939-_____) American billionaire
fashion designer, philanthropist, and business executive
Birth Name — Ralph Lifschitz

2013, *Arnaldo Anaya-Lucca,*
Creative Commons Attribution- Share Alike

Born in the Bronx, New York to Ashkenazi Jewish immigrants, his father
was a house painter. He attended day school, MTA then graduated from
DeWitt Clinton High School in 1957. He sold ties to classmates and
dreamed of becoming rich. Because of being teased over the sound of his
surname, he decided at age 16 that Lauren sounded better.[112] He
attended Baruch College studying business but dropped out after two
years, joining the Army from 1962-'64. He went with Brooks Brothers as
a sales assistant then worked as a salesman for a tie company. At age 26
he designed a wide necktie like he had seen worn by **Douglas
Fairbanks, Jr.**, but it was rejected by his employer, so he left to start his
own company, working out of a drawer in the Empire State Building,
taking rags and making them into ties, selling them to small shops.
When Neiman Marcus bought 1200, it was a major turning point for him.
In 1967, with backing of Manhattan clothier, **Norman Hilton**, he opened
his first store, now Polo.

Joey Lawrence (April 20, 1976-_____) American actor, singer and show game host

Birth Name — Joseph Lawrence Mignogna, Jr.

2012 at American Humane Association, State Farm, Creative Commons Attribution- Share Alike

Born in Philadelphia, Pennsylvania, he is the son of an insurance broker father and a former elementary school teacher mother. After graduating from Abington Friends School in Jenkintown, Pennsylvania he attended the University of Southern California. When Joey started acting he changed his last name to Lawrence, his middle name,[113] and the family followed. His first acting job was on a Cracker Jack commercial, and at age 5 he appeared on the *Tonight Show with Johnny Carson* where he sang, *Give My Regards to Broadway*. After guest spots on *Different Strokes* and *Silver Spoons* he won the role of Joey Donovan on the NBC sitcom, *Gimme a Break!* in 1983 which he kept until the series ended in 1987. He was also the voice of Oliver in Disney's *Oliver and Company* in 1988. Then from 1991 to '95 he starred in *Blossom* as Joey Russo. Other roles followed.

His two younger brothers Matthew and Andrew are also actors.

John Legend (December 18, 1978-_____) American singer, songwriter and actor
Birth Name — John Roger Stephens

2011 Citi Presents Evenings with Legends, *Sachyn Mital*, Creative Commons Attribution – Share Alike

Born in Springfield, Ohio, he is the son of a factory worker father and a seamstress mother. Off and on he was homeschooled, and he sang with his father in the church choir at the age of four. By seven he was playing piano. He entered high school at age 12, graduating in four years as salutatorian and was offered admission to Harvard and scholarships to Georgetown and Morehouse Universities. Instead, he attended the University of Pennsylvania, studying English and African-American literature. While in college he served as president of a co-ed jazz and pop a cappella group called Counterparts. A lead vocal with the group received critical acclaim putting it on a CD titled *The Best of Collegiate a Cappella*. He was also a member of prestigious groups there. Around this time he began performing in a number of shows around Philadelphia, then branching out to other major cities. He then signed to **Kanye West**'s label. Poet **J. Ivy** gave him the idea for his stage name, telling him he sounded like the legends, and calling him **John Legend**.[114]

118

Tea Leoni (February 25, 1966-_____) American actress and producer
Birth Name — Elizabeth Tea Pantaleoni

2007, *You Kill Me* Screening,
Gustavo Fernandez, Creative Commons Attribution, OTRS

Born in New York City to a corporate lawyer father and a dietitian mother, her paternal grandmother was a Polish-American film and stage actress named Helenka Adamowska Pantaleoni. She grew up in Inglewood, New Jersey and New York City, attending two private schools in Vermont. She also attended, but did not complete, Sarah Lawrence College in Yonkers. In 1988 she was cast as one of the members of *Angels 88*, to be an updated version of *Charlie's Angels* from the '70s. After production delays, the show was never aired. The next year Leoni was cast as Lisa DiNapoli in the NBC daytime soap opera, *Santa Barbara*. In 1991 she made her big-screen debut with a bit part in a comedy, *Switch;* then appeared briefly in *A League of Their Own*. By1998 she had a leading role in *Impact;* other major parts came soon. Her stage name is merely her middle name (a family tradition) and a shortening of her last.[115]

Sophia Loren (September 20, 1934-_____) Italian film actress
Birth Name — Sophia Vallani Scicolone

1969 Publicity Photo, Public Domain

Born in Rome, Italy, her father was a construction engineer of noble descent, Riccardo Scicolone, who refused to marry her mother, a piano teacher and aspiring actress, leaving her with no support, after having a second daughter with her, Maria, in 1938. Sciolone had two younger sons by another woman. The two girls lived with their grandmother in Pozzuoli near Naples, and after being wounded by shrapnel during WW II, the family moved into Naples, living with other relatives. After the war they returned to Pozzuoli, where Sophia's grandmother opened a pub in her living room. Her mother played piano there, and the sisters waited tables and washed dishes. At 14 she entered a beauty contest and was a finalist. Later she entered an acting class and was selected as an extra in *Quo Vadis* in 1951, launching her career. First credited as Sophia Lazzaro, she began using Sophia Loren as a stage name in *La Favorita* in 1952, which was a twist on the name of a Swiss actress, Märta Torén, suggested by producer Carlo Ponti, whom she married, according to a 2008 DVD.[116] She won an Oscar for her performance in *Two Women,* 1961.

Joe Louis (May 13, 1914 – April 12, 1981) American pro boxer, World Heavyweight Champion, 1937-1949
Birth Name — Joseph Louis Barrow

1949, Public Domain

Born near Lafayette, Alabama, Joe was the seventh of eight children of sharecropper parents who were both children of former slaves. He weighed a whopping 11 pounds at birth. His dad was committed to a mental institution at his age two. Louis had a speech impediment, speaking very little until about age six. Being told that her husband was dead when he really was not, his mother remarried four years later. Shaken by the local KKK, in 1926 the family moved to the Black Bottom neighborhood of Detroit. His mother got him a violin, but Joe was spending time at the youth center, his boxing gloves allegedly in his violin case. Legend has it that the night of his first fight at age 17, Joe wrote his name so large that there was no room for his last name, and he became known as Joe Louis throughout his boxing career.[117] The next year, 1933, at age 18, he won the Detroit Area Golden Gloves Novice Division championship. He went on to World Heavyweight Champ. My father trained under his original trainer, **Jack Blackburn**, knocking him out. My dad, offered a pro boxing career, turned it down.

Courtney Love (July 9, 1964-_____) American alternative rock singer, songwriter, musician, actress, and visual artist
Birth Name — Courtney (or Love) Michelle Harrison

1995, Melbourne, Australia, *Andrzej Liguz*,
OTRS Permission

Courtney was born in San Francisco, California to a publisher father who briefly managed the **Grateful Dead**, and physiotherapist mother, daughter of novelist **Paula Fox** and possibly fathered by **Marlon Brando**. Her parents divorced in 1969. The next year they moved to a commune in rural Oregon. Later she was adopted by her stepfather, Frank Rodriguez. Going to school in Eugene was a struggle. She was diagnosed with mild autism. In '72, her mother filed for divorce moving to New Zealand. Courtney enrolled in college, but was sent back to Oregon to live with Rodriguez. Rejected for the Mickey Mouse Club at 12, she took a film class but was arrested at 14 for shoplifting. After several foster homes she worked as a stripper in Portland, and later worked as an exotic dancer in other countries, and she chose to be called Courtney Love, because her mother had called her that.[118] She was prolific in the 1990s, fronting **Hole**. Now she wants to be called Michelle Harrison.

Myrna Loy (August 2, 1905-December 13, 1993) American film, television and stage actress
Birth Name — Myrna Adele Williams

C. 1925 Publicity Photo, Public Domain

Born in Helena, Montana to a rancher father who was the son of Welsh immigrants, her mother nearly died from pneumonia at her age seven, and her father sent Myrna with her to La Holla, California, where they purchased real estate, some of which was later sold to **Charlie Chaplin**. There Loy began dancing lessons. But her father did not want to relocate there so they returned to Montana. After her father's death in 1918, they moved back to Southern California where her teachers persuaded Myrna to take theatrical arts. At age 15 she began appearing in local stage productions. After being the subject of an elegant sculpture at her school, she left and went to work at Grauman's Egyptian Theater. Her photos were noticed by **Rudolph Valentino** who was seeking a leading lady for *Corba*. Though not selected, she was cast as a chorus girl in *Pretty Ladies* (1925). Her photos in a fan magazine led to a Warner Brothers contract and her name was changed to Myrna Loy.[119] Though silent roles cast her as a vamp, later ones even included *The Best Years of Our Lives* (1946).

Ludicrous (September 11, 1977-_____) American rapper, entrepreneur and actor
Birth Name — Christopher Brian Bridges

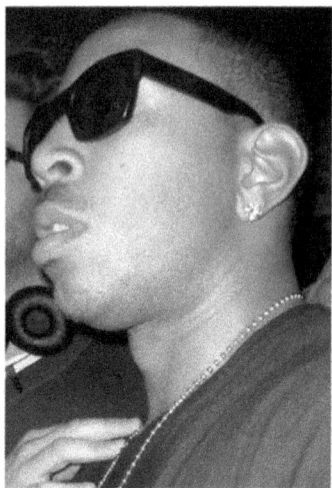

2011 at Strobe Live, Miami Beach, *Secret*
Creative Commons Attributions- Share Alike

Christopher was an only child born in Champlain, Illinois. Later he moved to the Chicago area, then to Centerville, Virginia before moving to Atlanta where he graduated from Banneker High in 1995; then enrolled in Georgia State University, studying music management. He was said to have written his first rap song at age nine, and by age 12 he was in a rap band. He was an intern and then a DJ on Atlanta's Hot 97.5, now Hot 107.9, using the handle Chris Lova Lova. He collaborated with **Timbaland** on *Phat Rabbit* on his album *Tim's Bio: Life from da Bassment,* later included on Ludicrous' debut LP album, *Back for the First Time.* He told an MTV interviewer that he based his stage name on his "split personality," which he described as being "ridiculous and ludicrous."[120] He first appeared on *Saturday Night Live* as a guest, and has since returned. Though controversial, he has gained immense popularity in his field, recording many top selling albums.

Elle Macpherson (March 29, 1964-_____) Australian businesswoman, television host, model and actress
Birth Name — Eleanor Nancy Gow

2011 Invisible Zink Promo, Sydney, Australia, *Eva Rinaldi,* Creative Commons Attribution- Share Alike

Born in Killara, New South Wales, she is the daughter of an entrepreneur and sound engineer father and a mother who was a nurse. Her parents divorced at her age ten. Later her mother remarried and a clerical mistake at the school changed her surname from Gow to Macpherson (her stepfather's name).[121]

She grew up and attended high school in East Lindfield; then traveled to the U.S. doing modeling to earn money for law books, but only studied law for one year at the University of Sydney before moving to New York and signing with Click Modeling Agency in 1982, beginning by doing a TV commercial for Tab. Soon she was on the cover of *Cosmopolitan, Elle, Vogue, Harper's Bazaar, Time* and others. But *Sports Illustrated Swimsuit Edition* opened more doors, leading to a nude appearance in the movie *Sirens* in 1994, then again in *Playboy.*

Lee Majors (April 23, 1939-_____) American television, film and voice actor

Birth Name — Harvey Lee Yeary

1972 ABS Photo, Public Domain

Born in Wyandotte, Michigan, his father was killed in an accident prior to his birth and his mother in another accident when he was 1 year old. Adopted by an uncle and aunt at age 2, he moved to Middlesboro, Kentucky. In high school he participated in football, graduating in 1957 with a scholarship to Indiana University then transferred to East Kentucky University in 1959. After only one football game there he suffered a back injury which ended his college football career. He then turned to acting, being cast in plays at the Pioneer Playhouse in Danville, Kentucky. He graduated in 1962 with a degree in History and Physical Education. He was invited to try out for the St. Louis Cardinals football team, but instead moved to Los Angeles, taking a job as Recreational Director of the North Hollywood Park. There he met **Dick Clayton** who had been **James Dean**'s agent, who got him into acting school at MGM. After one year he got small roles. He took his stage name from his friend, Coach **Johnny Majors**,[122] from near my home in Middle Tennessee. He is best known for roles in *Big Valley, the Six Million Dollar Man* and *Fall Guy*.

Barry Manilow (June 17, 1943-_____) American singer-songwriter and producer
Birth Name — Barry Alan Pincus

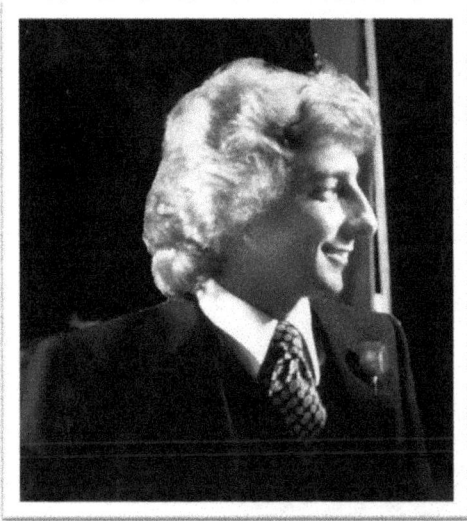

1979 Photo by *Alan Light*, CCA

Born in Brooklyn, New York, his mother was Jewish and his father Irish American with distant Jewish descent. Barry adopted his mother's maiden name of Manilow at the time of his bar mitzvah.[123] Growing up in the Williamsburg section of Brooklyn, he graduated high school in 1961, briefly attending the City College of New York before entering the New York College of Music, working for CBS to pay expenses. After a brief marriage, he entered Julliard performing arts school. In 1964, Manilow wrote an entire new score for the melodrama *The Drunkard*, though only asked to rearrange the original music. **Bro Herrod** used his composition in the Off-Broadway musical which played for eight years. He then began working as a pianist, producer and arranger, also writing jingles for State Farm Insurance, Band-Aid, Kentucky Fried Chicken, Pepsi Cola, Polaroid and the famed McDonalds "You Deserve a Break Today" campaign. Songs like *Mandy, Can't Smile Without You* and *Copacabana* soared to the top of the pop charts.

Marilyn Manson (January 5, 1969-_____) American musician, songwriter, multi-instrumentalist, actor, painter, multimedia artist, and former music journalist

Birth Name — Brian Hugh Warner

2010, At Quart Festival Sike, Kristiansand, Norway, *Rockman,*
Creative Commons Attribution- Share Alike

Born in Canton, Ohio, he attended Heritage Christian School to tenth grade. There they showed students the music they were NOT supposed to listen to, and he fell in love with that music. He transferred to and graduated from Glen Oak High in 1987. After moving to Fort Lauderdale, Florida, he enrolled at Broward Community College in 1990. There he wrote articles for the music magazine *25th Parallel*. He had met several of the musicians which would comprise his band. First he and **Scott Putesky** formed Marilyn Manson and the Spooky Kids in 1989, later shortening the name to only Marilyn Manson, which Warner came up with by combining the names of **Marilyn Monroe** with psychotic cult leader **Charles Manson**.[124] It is also the name which he chose to go by professionally. The band developed a heavy metal style, first playing clubs, later making a hit on MTV, and having 2 platinum albums, 3 gold.

Bruno Mars (October 8, 1985-_____) American singer, songwriter, record producer, voice actor, and choreographer
Birth Name — Peter Gene Hernandez

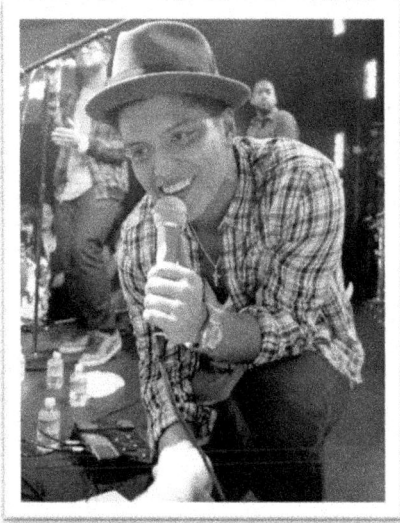

2010, Las Vegas, *Chrizta T*,
Creative Commons Attribution-Share Alike

Born in Honolulu, Hawaii, he is of mixed race, his father being half-Puerto-Rican and half Ashkenazi Jewish, and his mother of Filipino descent with distant Spanish ancestry. Mars was raised in Waikiki with both parents being musical. At age two he was nicknamed Bruno by his father because of his resemblance to pro wrestler Bruno Sammartino.[125] According to Bruno, "Mars came up because a lot of girls say I'm out of this world!"

While very young, he was exposed to all sorts of music from reggae to rock and pop. His mom danced and sang and his dad was a musician, plus an uncle was an Elvis impersonator. Bruno started performing songs by **Michael Jackson** and others on stage at age three. By four, he performed five days a week. In 1990 he was featured on *MidWeek* as Little Elvis. After high school, moving to LA, he was signed by *Motown*.

129

Dean Martin (June 7, 1917 – December 25, 1995) American singer, actor, comedian and film producer
Birth Name — Dino Paul Crocetti

1960 Publicity Photo, Public Domain

Born in Steubenville, Ohio to an Italian father and Italian-American mother, his first language was actually an Italian dialect, and he didn't speak any English until he started school at age five, and was bullied in school for his broken English. Little did these children realize that he would become one of the most endearing entertainers of the 20th century. Dropping out of school in the 10th grade, he became a bootlegger, boxed as a welterweight, getting a broken nose and many scars and bruises, served as a speakeasy croupier; working in an illegal casino behind a tobacco shop where he started as a stock boy. At the same time he started singing with bands as Dino Martini, after the operatic singer, Nino Martini. In the early 1940s he started singing for bandleader **Sammy Watkins**, who suggested he change his name to Dean Martin.[126] Meeting **Jerry Lewis** in a New York Club later and forming a music-comedy team was the turning point in his career.

Ricky Martin (December 24, 1971-_____) Puerto Rican, American, Spanish singer, songwriter, actor and author
Birth Name — Enrique Martin Morales

2014, Sidney Australia, *Eva Rinaldi,* Creative Commons Attribution-Share Alike

Born in San Juan, Puerto Pico to a psychologist father and accountant mother, his parents divorced at his age two and he spent much of his childhood between his father's home and that of his paternal grandparents nearby. He was a Roman Catholic altar boy, and started singing at age six. His mother's family was musically inclined, and his maternal grandfather was a poet, which inspired his to write songs. He began his career at age 12 with an all boy pop group, **Menudo.** After five years he released several Spanish solo albums during the 1990s. He also did stage acting in Mexico, achieving minor fame there. In 1994 he starred in the American soap Opera, General Hospital as a Puerto Rican singer. After recording several Spanish albums, he performed on the Grammy Award show in 1999, putting Latin pop music on the American market. Soon, he released *Livin' La Viva Loca*, which met with great success. Martin was also a family name, and he changed his first name (Enrique) to Ricky after being estranged from his father.[127]

George Michael (June 25, 1963-_____) English singer, songwriter, instrumentalist and record producer
Birth Name — Georgios Panayiotou

2007, 25 Live, Portland, *Joe Web*,
Creative Commons Attribution- Share Alike

Classified as a "Blue-eyed soul singer," George was born in North London to a Greek restaurateur father who also changed his name, and an English dancer mother. He spent most of his childhood in Kingsbury in North West London. While he was a young teen, the family moved to Radlett, Hertfordshire. Later he bartended his future **Wham!** partner **Andrew Ridgeley**. George also did street performing on the London Underground. He began as a DJ performing in clubs and local schools. He first found real success in **Wham!** with Ridgeley in 1981, their first album hitting number one in the UK, and the second making number one in the U.S. George Michael is the Anglicized version of his name which he has used since the early 1980s.[128] Later he embarked on a solo career. Michael is one of the world's best loved music artists, selling more than 100 million records worldwide since 2010 alone, and winning numerous music awards in his 30-year career.

Bret Michaels (March 15, 1963-_____) American singer, song-writer, musician, actor, director, producer, and reality TV personality
Birth Name — Bret Michael Sychak

2008, with Poison,
Moondance Jam, Walker, Minnesota, Creative Commons Attribution

Born in Butler, Pennsylvania, he was diagnosed with type one diabetes at the age of six and hospitalized for three weeks (something he didn't announce until years later after a going into insulin shock on stage). He began playing guitar as a teen, and with **Rikki Rockett, Bobby Dahl** and **David Basselman**, then **Matt Smith**, formed the band that would eventually become **Poison** after moving to Los Angeles in 1984. David had left the band before the move, then Mike left and was replaced by **C.C. DeVille**. Even before he left Pennsylvania, he changed his name to Michaels,[129] dropping his surname and adding the 's' to his middle name. Michaels reached fame as lead singer for the Glam metal group, but began doing solos in the late '90s. Several bands have influenced his style including **Kiss, AC/DC** and **Aerosmith**.

He is now front man for the Bret Michaels Band.

Nicki Minaj(December 8, 1982-_____) Trinidadian-born American rapper, singer, songwriter and actress
Birth Name — Onika Tanya Maraj

2013 at BET Awards, *Fer Morrell,* Creative Commons Attribution- Share Alike

Born in St. James Trinidad and Tobago, her father was a financial executive and her mother had worked as a foreign exchange teller and gospel singer. Sadly, her father was an alcoholic and drug addict who had tried to kill her mother. As a small child she lived with her grandmother. Then at age five she moved with her mother to Queens, New York. In middle school she played the clarinet. At LaGuardia High School in Manhattan she studied acting. Then she was cast in the Off-Broadway play *In Case You Forgot* in 2001. Fired from several jobs, she worked as a Wall Street assistant. In 2007 she signed with the Brooklyn group, **Full Force**, rapping with the **Hoodstars** who recorded *Don't Mess With Me*. Leaving the group, she posted her songs on MySpace, sending some to music execs. **Fendi** signed her to a 180-day Dirty Money Records contract as Nicki (nickname) Maraj, but she changed it to Nicki Manaj.[130] She released *Prime Time is Over* in 2007 and *Second is Free* in 2008, leading to a top award.

Helen Mirren (July 26, 1945-_____) English actor
Birth Name — Ilyena Lydia Vasilievna Mirinov

2014, London, MBI Film Awards, *See Li*,
Creative Commons Attribution

Mirren was born in London to a Russian father whose father was a colonel in the Russian Army and English mother. Helen's father Anglicized the family name to Mirren in the 1950s.[131]

She attended St. Bernard's High School for Girls where she acted in school plays, then New College of Speech and Drama in London. She was accepted for National Youth Theater at the age of 18. By age 20 she was playing Cleopatra in their production of *Antony and Cleopatra*.

She debuted in film in the 1960s, and has starred in many prominent movies including *Caligula, Excalibur, Calendar Girls* and *The Last Station*. In recent years she has played both Queen Elizabeth I and Queen Elizabeth II, and has won an Academy Award for Best Actress, 4 BAFTs, 3 Golden Globes, 4 Emmy Awards, 2 Cannes Film Festival Best Actress Awards, and 1 Tony Award. In 2003 she received a Damehood.

Marilyn Monroe (June 1, 1926 – August 5, 1962) American actress, model, singer and sex symbol
Birth Name — Norma Jeane Mortenson

1950s Photo, Public Domain

Born in Los Angeles County Hospital with her father listed as Martin Mortenson, her mother's estranged husband, her name was soon changed to Baker, her mother's surname from her first husband. Because of her mother's instability, Marilyn was declared a ward of the state, and she spent much time in foster homes. Her guardian, Grace McGee created in Marilyn a love of the cinema, and told her that she would one day become a movie star. Childhood abuse caused behavioral problems, hyper-sexuality and drug abuse. At her aunt's home she met and married Jim Dougherty, who worked as a Merchant Marine and she, at a Radioplane Munitions Factory. David Conover of the Army Air Force's First Motion Picture Unit was sent to the factory by his C.O., **Ronald Reagan**. He took photos of her which appeared in *Yank Army Weekly* and encouraged her to model. **Ben Lyon** of 20th Century Fox signed her, and a new name was requested. After several variations, Marilyn (for Marilyn Miller) Monroe (her mother's maiden name) was chosen.[132]

Clayton Moore (September 14, 1914- December 28, 1999) American actor best known for playing the Lone Ranger
Birth Name — Jack Carlton Moore

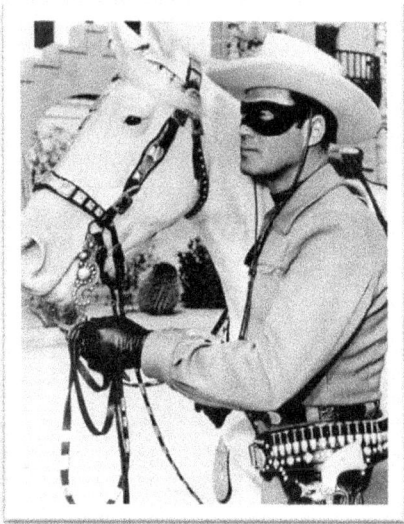

1965 as Lone Ranger, Public Domain

Born in Chicago, Moore was a circus acrobat by age 8. After graduating high school, he worked as a successful model before moving to Hollywood in the late 1930s. According to his 1998 autobiography, *I Was That Masked Man,* about 1940, producer **Edward Small** persuaded him adopt the stage name "Clayton" Moore.[133] Occasionally playing in B Westerns for Republic and Columbia, Moore served in the Army during World War II and made training films with the First Motion Picture Unit.

In 1949, **George Trendle**, creator-producer of the *Lone Ranger* radio show spotted him in the *Ghost of Zorro* serial, and hired Moore to star in his upcoming television version. Strangely, he trained his voice to sound like the one in the radio version, lowering it even more, so it was not originally his sound. Moore and co-star, **Jay Silverheels,** made history as the stars of the first western series made specifically for television. The show soon became the top rated show on ABC, winning an Emmy.

Demi Moore (November 11, 1962-_____) American actress, film maker, former songwriter, and model
Birth Name — Demetria Guynes

2009 Pre-Inaugural Party, *Cliff,* CCA

Born in Roswell, New Mexico, her biological father, Airman Charles Harmon, Sr., left her mother after a two-month marriage, before she was born. When Demi (nickname) was three months old, her mother married Dan Guynes, who raised her before committing suicide in October, 1980 at the age of 37, two years after separating from Demi's mother. When she married actor **Freddy Moore** in 1980, Demi chose to take her married name as her stage name[134] and kept it after the divorce and into her future marriages to **Bruce Willis** and **Ashton Kutcher**, from both of whom she is also divorced. Moore dropped out of high school at age 16 to pursue a career in acting, appearing nude in *Oui Magazine* in 1961. Like many other actresses, this seemed to spark her career, as she made her film debut that same year on the ABC soap opera, *General Hospital*, and gained recognition for work in films within five years. In 1990, *Ghost*, with **Patrick Swayze**, earned her a Golden Globe nomination. Other huge box-office successes followed in the 1990s.

Dinty Moore (1869-December 25, 1952) Irish-American restaurant owner
Birth Name—James A. Moore, Jr.

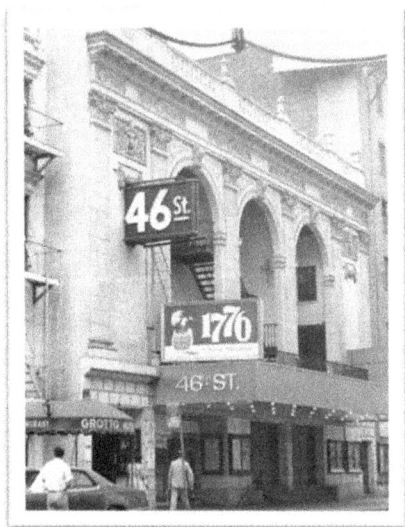

Dinty Moore's Restaurant, Pub. D.

This name has been used by businesses and persons in many professions. Who originated it? In 1913 a New York cartoonist, George McManus, created a comic strip titled *Bringing Up Father* about a struggling working class Irish couple, *Jiggs and Maggie,* who won the Irish sweepstakes. It became one of the most successful syndicated cartoon strips of all time—for 87 years! One of Jigs' friends was a tavern owner named Dinty Moore. A friend of McManus, James Moore, claimed that the character of Dinty was based on him, and changed his name; putting it on his restaurant in Manhattan in 1914.[135] Irish stew was popular there. Several other Dinty Moore restaurants popped up around the country, including one in my home-town of McMinnville, Tennessee. In the 1930s a Minneapolis meat retailer registered the name. Hormel Foods bought the trademark and promoted its own beef stew under the Dinty Moore brand...I loved it as a child.

139

Julianne Moore (December 3, 1960-_____) American actress and children's author
Birth Name — Julie Anne Smith

2009, Festival de Venise, *Nicholas Genin*, Collective Commons Attribution- Share Alike

She was born in Fort Brag, North Carolina, where her father, Peter Moore Smith was an Army paratrooper, who later became a colonel and military judge. Her mother, Anne, was a psychiatrist and social worker from Scotland who immigrated as a child in 1950. The family moved a lot during her youth, around the U.S. and even to Panama, and Germany, where she acted in plays and loved to read. In 1983 she earned a BFA in Theater from the Boston University and moved to New York City, registering in Actor's Equity. She found that others were already registered with her name and chose the stage name Julianne Moore, putting together her first and middle names and using her father's middle name as her surname.[136]After several TV appearances she was cast in CBS's *As the World Turns* in 1985, kicking off her popularity. Starring in many movies, she has received three Oscar nominations and a *Volpi Cup* in Venice and *Silver Bear* for Best Actress in Berlin.

Grandma Moses (September 7, 1860 – December 13, 1961) American folk artist
Birth Name — Anna Mary Robertson

1953 Photo, Public Domain

Born in Greenwich, New York she was the third child of ten. Her father ran a flax mill and was a farmer. The one-room school which she briefly attended as a child is now the Bennington Museum in Vermont and has the largest collection of her works in the U.S. She first painted as a child using lemon and grape to make colors for what she called "lambscapes." She also used ground ochre, grass, flour paste, slack lime and sawdust. Leaving home at age 12, she worked for a wealthy neighbors doing farm choirs. One of the families saw that she was interested in their Currier and Ives prints, and bought chalk and wax crayons so she could create her own art work. At age 27 she married one of the other farm workers named Thomas Salmon Moses. They established a home near Staunton Virginia, having 10 children, 5 of whom survived. She had done embroidery, but after her husband's death, because of her arthritis, her sister suggested that she paint. Her unique work caught on. This spurred her career in her 70's. The press dubbed her "Grandma Moses."[137]

Jonathan Rhys Meyers (July 27, 1977-_____) Irish actor
Birth Name — Jonathan Michael Francis O'Keefe

2013, Caboug, *Ellen Nivrae,*
Creative Commons Attribution

Born in Dublin, Ireland, he is the son of a musician, and has three brothers who are also professional musicians. After his parents separated at his age three, his mother raised him and his brother Alan in a council flat in Cork while their other brothers went to live with his father and his parents. His mother was a heavy drinker and they lived in poverty. His family being traditionally Catholic, he briefly attended North Monastery Christian Brothers School, but was expelled at age 16. Working at a pool hall he lived in the home of Christopher Croft who was convicted of abusing another boy and sentenced to one year in prison. When turned down for an acting role he was encouraged to pursue acting and was cast in *A Man of Importance* (1994), then *Michael Collins* in 1996, and *Ride with the Devil* in 1999, along with several other roles in film and TV. He said his name was boring, concocting his stage name using Myers, his mother's maiden name.[138] He is well known for playing in **Woody Allen**'s *Match Point* and his TV role as **Elvis Presley** which won a Golden Globe. From 2007 to '10 he was wildly popular in Showtime's *Henry VIII.*

142

Nita Naldi (November 13, 1894 – February 17, 1961) American silent
film actress and femme fatale
Birth Name — Mary Dooley

1920s Publicity Photo, Public Domain

Before there was *Fatal Attraction* with **Glenn Close**, or even *The Killers*
with **Ava Gardner**, there was Nita Naldi. Born in New York City in 1894
to working class Irish parents, she was named for her great aunt Mary
Nonna Dunphy founder of the Academy of Holy Angels in Ft. Lee, New
Jersey, which she attended as a teen. Her mother died at her age 20, and
she had to seek employment which she found as a model, later entering
vaudeville. She debuted on Broadway as a chorus girl in *Passing Show of
1918,* which led to hiring for the *Ziegfeld Follies*. That's when she changed
her name to Nita Naldi in honor of a childhood friend, Florence
Rinaldi.[139] Next, famed producer **William A. Brady** cast her in his play,
Opportunity in 1920. Offered a role in a silent film by **Johnny Dooley**, she
pulled out when she realized that he had a romantic interest in another
woman. **Owen Moore** then gave her a role in *A Divorce of Convenience*.
She was then launched into a film career including **DeMille's** original
Ten Commandments. She was often cast as a vamp (femme fatale).

Annie Oakley (August 13, 1860 - November 3, 1926) American
sharpshooter and exhibition shooter
Birth Name — Phoebe Ann Mosey

1880s Cabinet Card, Public Domain

Annie was born to Quaker parents in a log cabin in Darke County, Ohio.
Although there has been much debate as to her family name, the Annie
Oakley Association has certified that it was Mosey, not Moses. She had 8
siblings. Her father died at her age 5 and Annie began hunting at 8.
Because of poverty and her father's death Annie was placed in an
infirmary at age 9, and had little schooling in childhood. She was soon
bound out to a family who kept her in near slavery, mentally and
physically abusing her. 2 years later, she ran away. She continued hunting and selling game to restaurants. At 15 she returned to her mother
and paid off her mortgage. Her shooting skill became well known. In
1875 traveling show marksman **Frank Butler** placed a $100 bet per side
($2,148 today) that he could beat any challenger in Cincinnati. 15-year-
old Annie beat him after the 25th shot. A year later the two were married
and she changed her name to Annie Oakley when they began performing together.[140] In 1885 they joined **Buffalo Bill's Wild West** show.

George Orwell (25 June 1903 – 21 January 1950) English novelist, essayist, journalist and critic
Birth Name — Eric Arthur Blair

1943, Press Card Photo, Public Domain

Orwell was born in Motihari, in British India (present-day Bihar). His father worked in the Indian Civil Service. At his age two, his mother, who had grown up in Burma left, taking him and his two older sisters to England, settling in Oxfordshire, where he attended a convent school. Later, in Shiplake he met Jacintha Buddicom with whom he wrote poetry. Then he attended St. Cyprian's School in East Sussex where he met **Cyril Connolly** who became a noted writer who later as editor of *Horizon*, published several of his essays. At this school he wrote many poems which were published. He is noted for literary criticism and support of democratic socialism. As for 'Orwell' he used this after the River Orwell which ran through Ipswich in England. 'George,' according to his biography, was chosen because such a first name is a normal one for an Englishman. According to Eleanor Jaques, he announced, "I'm going to call myself George Orwell, because it's a good round English name." (p. 126).[141] He is best known for writing *Animal Farm* and *1984*.

Buck Owens (August 12, 1929-March 25, 2006) American musician, singer, songwriter and band leader
Birth Name — Alvis Edgar Owens, Jr.

1977, Warner Bros, Rec., Pub. Dom.

Owens was born in Sherman, Texas, to a farm family. *About Buck*, a biography by **Rich McKienzle**, has the following: "'Buck' was a donkey on the Owens farm. When Alvis Jr. was three or four years old, he walked into the house and announced that his name also was 'Buck.' That was fine with the family, and the boy's name was Buck from then on."[142] The family moved to Mesa, Arizona, during the Depression in 1937. At age 16, Buck co-hosted a radio show called *Buck and the Britt*. In the late 1940s as a truck driver he went to California and was impressed with Bakersfield. After his marriage, he settled there in 1951. Soon he was going into Hollywood playing back up on Capitol Records for the likes of **Tennessee Ernie Ford, Sonny James, Del Reeves, Faron Young** and others. His first solo record was a rockabilly song called *Hot Dog* on the Pep Label under the name Corky Jones. After meeting **Don Rich** in 1958, his career took off, having 21 number one hits then co-hosting *Hee-Haw*, the longest running country music variety show of all time.

146

Minnie Pearl (October 25, 1912 – March 4, 1996) American country comedian and television star
Birth Name — Sarah Ophelia Colley

1965 Publicity Photo, Public Domain

Born in Centerville in Southwest-Middle-Tennessee, Sarah was the daughter of a prosperous lumberman. She graduated from Ward-Belmont College, now Belmont University, the most prestigious school in Nashville for young ladies then, where her major was theater, and dance was an interest. After graduation she taught dance for many years; then produced and directed plays for Wayne P. Sewell Production Company around the southeastern U.S. While producing a play in Baileyton, Alabama she met a mountain woman whose style and talk were the basis for her famous character.[143] Her first stage appearance as Minnie Pearl was in 1939 in Aiken, South Carolina, where she purchased her famous hat at a department store right before the show. The next year producers at WSM radio saw her perform at a bankers' convention and invited her to appear on the *Grand Ole Opry* on 30 November 1940 for the first time. One of my aunts bore a striking resemblance to her, and they had their picture taken together. I had the pleasure of seeing her in person twice; once up very close, in my hometown of McMinnville.

147

Katy Perry (October 25, 1984-_____) American singer, songwriter and actress

Birth Name—Katheryn Elizabeth Hudson

2014 ARIA Music Awards, *Eva Rinaldi*, Creative Commons Attribution- Share Alike

Katy was born in Santa Barbara, California to Pentecostal pastor parents, both converted after being "wild youths." Her mother is the sister of film director **Frank Perry**. Moving a lot, her parents set up churches and she attended Christian schools, finally settling again in Santa Barbara. They struggled financially, sometimes using food stamps and supplies from church food banks. Her parents were strict, and she was encouraged to listen to only gospel music as a youth. She began singing at age nine in her parents' ministry. At 13, she was given her first guitar. She got a GED at 15, leaving school, studying opera and singing. Catching the attention of Nashville producers, she was signed to Red Hill Records, originally as a gospel artist, Katy Hudson. Transitioning to secular music, she changed to her mother's maiden name to avoid confusion with **Kate Hudson**, daughter of actress **Goldie Hawn**.[144] She signed with Capitol Records and in 2008 her career took off with the release of *I Kissed a Girl* and *Hot and Cold*. *Teenage Dream* and *Firework* soared high.

Bernadette Peters (February 28, 1948-_____) American actor, singer and children's book author
Birth Name — Bernadette Lazzara

1974 in *Mack and Mable,* Public Domain

Born to a Sicilian American family in Queens, New York, her father drove a delivery truck and her mother started her in show business by putting her on the TV show *Juvenile Jury* at age 3 ½ and two other shows at age 5. She didn't look Italian, and her father's name was Peter, so her surname was changed to Peters when she was very young to discourage ethnic typecasting, and she soon began appearing in local stage shows.[145] At age 9, she got an actor's Equity Card. Over the past five decades her career has taken her to the top of her field. She has starred in musical theater, big screen movies and television, as well as solo performances and concerts. A critically acclaimed Broadway performer, she has been nominated for seven Tony Awards, winning two and nine Drama Desk Awards, winning three. Four of the Broadway plays in which she has starred have won Grammys. Garnering high praise for early TV shows, she has won three Emmys and four Golden Globe Awards.

Slim Pickens (June 29, 1919 – December 8, 1983) American rodeo performer, film and television comedy actor
Birth Name — Louis Burton Lindley, Jr.

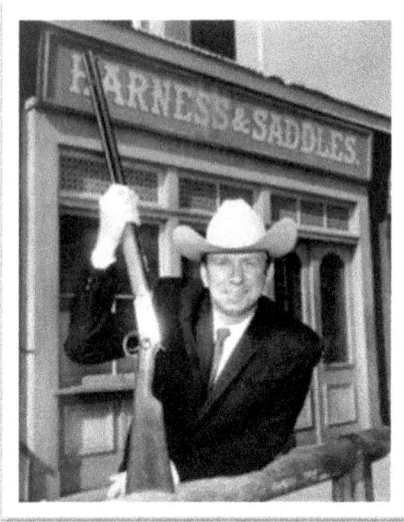

1972 Photo, Public Domain

Born in Kingsbury, California, his dad was a dairy farmer born in Texas. An excellent horse rider from childhood, Louis, Jr. was called Bert by his family and friends. Bored of dairy farming in his early teens he began making money riding broncs and roping steers. Against his father's will, he went to compete in a rodeo where the manager told him there would be "slim pickin's" for him. To keep his father from finding out that he was competing he entered his name as Slim Pickens and won $400 that day.[146] Hanging around at the rodeo, when a clown no-showed, Pickens filled in. He loved it and made it full-time, dressing in Mexican Torero clothes, working as a rodeo clown bull fighter in several local venues. He got his first film role with **Errol Flynn** in *Rocky Mountain* (1950). He played in more than 150 movies and TV series, being remembered most for such films as *Stage Coach*, with **Ann Margaret** and **Bing Crosby**, *The Getaway* with **Steve McQueen** and *Blazing Saddles*.

Pink (September 8, 1979-_____) American singer, songwriter and actress

Birth Name — Alecia Beth Moore

Pink, Public Domain Image

Moore was born in Doyelstown, Pennsylvania to a Vietnam Veteran, insurance salesman, Catholic father and a mother of Lithuanian Jewish descent. Pink had asthma as a child, and her parents divorced before her age 10. She developed her voice early and joined her first band in high school. She wrote song lyrics as a teen which reflected her complex, deep moods. Beginning performing in Philadelphia clubs at age 14, she chose Pink as a stage name at that time. Some said it was because she had a habit of blushing when she got embarrassed. Actually she took the name from the character "Mr. Pink," which friends said she resembled, in the movie *Reservoir Dogs*, which she saw as a young teen.[147] Pink dropped out of high school, getting her GED in 1998.

An MCA exec took note of her and a group took her, later another. She was determined to be her own person, and released her first solo album as Pink in 2000. It was certified double platinum with two top-10 hits.

Pitbull (January 15, 1981-_____) American rapper
Birth Name — Armando Christian Perez

2012, Sydney Australia, *Eva Rinaldi,*
Creative Commons Attribution, Share Alike

Born to Cuban immigrants who were not citizens, by age three he could recite the works of Cuban poet Jose Marti, a national hero there. He was influenced by the Miami bass genre of music. His parents separated when he was young and he was raised by his mother, and spent some time with a foster family in Roswell, Georgia. After graduating from high school in Miami he concentrated on a career as a rapper.

In his own words, he chose his stage name because pitbulls "bite to lock. The dog is too stupid to lose. And they're outlawed in Dade County. They're basically everything that I am. It's been a constant fight."[148]

He was first featured on the **Lil John** album, *Kids of Crunk* in 2002; then *Oye* was on the soundtrack *2 Fast 2 Furious* the next year. In 2004 he released his debut album, *M.I.A.M.I.* with the single *Culo*, and he was rolling! His 2011 album *Planet Pit* had the hit single *Give Me Everything*.

152

Natalie Portman   Israeli-born American actress, producer and director with dual citizenship
Birth Name — Natalie Herschlag

2015, Cannes Film Festival, *George Biard,*
Creative Commons Attribution- Share Alike, OTRS

Born in Jerusalem, she is the only child of an Israeli fertility specialist father of Romanian and Polish Jewish heritage and American mother who works as her agent. Her parents met at a Jewish student center at Ohio State University and were married in Israel. At her age three they moved to Washington DC and later, Connecticut, then Long Island, New York. Her father received medical training in the States. In DC Natalie attended Jewish day school and learned to speak Hebrew. On Long Island, she attended a Jewish elementary school and graduated from Syosset High, a public school. She studied ballet and dance then Creative and Performing Arts at Wheatley Heights. During the early '90s she had roles in the films *Heat, Everyone Says I Love You* and *Mars Attacks*. Natalie chose her grandmother's maiden name when she landed her first role in *Leon the Professional* in 1994.[149] This was to protect her privacy and that of her family. Then came *Star Wars* and *Closer*. In 2003 she graduated from Harvard; then went to Israel to take graduate courses.

will.i.am (March 15, 1975-_____) American singer, songwriter, rapper, entrepreneur, actor, musician, record producer, philanthropist
Birth Name—William James Adams, Jr.

2012 Hollywood, © *Glenn Francis,* www.PacificProDigital.com, Creative Commons Attribution- Share Alike

Proof positive of a modern "Rags-to-riches" story, Will was born in Eastside Los Angeles and grew up in Estrada Courts housing project never knowing his father. What he had going for him was a mother who encouraged him not to conform to the tendencies of the other youth in his neighborhood, who sent him to public school in affluent West Los Angeles. In Palisades Charter High he became friends with Alan Pinada who goes by the stage name **apl.de.ap**, a future member of the **Black Eyed Peas**. Along with three other members they formed the rap group **Alban Klan**, which **Eazy-E** signed to his label, Ruthless Records, in 1992. After **Eazy-E**'s tragic death the group's name was changed to the **Black Eyed Peas**. Originally called Will X1, following the example of **alp.de.ap**, he changed his name to will.i.am—likely because it conformed and sounded more awesome.[150] The group has won 7 Grammys, 8 American Music Awards, a Billboard Music Award, 2 MTA Video Awards, etc.

Wolfgang Puck (July 8, 1949-_____) Austrian-born American celebrity chef, restaurateur, and occasional actor
Birth Name — Wolfgang Johannes Topfschnig

2012, Los Angeles, © *Glenn Francis,* www.PacificProDigital.com Creative Commons Attribution- Share Alike

Born in Sankt Veit an der Glan, Carinthia, Austria, Puck learned cooking from his mother, who sometimes worked as a pastry chef. After apprentice training, he moved to the United States in 1973 at age 24. After two years at La Tour in Indianapolis, he moved to Los Angeles to become chef and part owner at Ma Maison restaurant. In 1981 he published a cookbook titled *Modern French Cooking for the American Kitchen* based on his receipts at the restaurant then the next year he and **Barbara Lazaroff** opened a restaurant on the Sunset Strip called Spago. 15 years later they opened another one by the same name in Beverly Hills, which has been recognized as one of the top 40 restaurants in the U.S. Though he says his real name is Puck, it was definitely changed legally by him. According John F. Mariani's book, *How Italian Food Conquered the World*, he "changed his name to the sprightlier Wolfgang Puck."[151] His companies include restaurants, catering services and books.

Della Reese (July 6, 1931-_____) American singer, actress, past-game show panelist and ordained minister
Birth Name — Delloreese Patricia Early

1977 Publicity Photo, Public Domain

Born in historic Black Bottom in Detroit, Michigan, her father was an African American steel worker and her mother was a Native American Cherokee cook. Her mother had children earlier, but none lived with her after Della's birth, so she grew up like an only child. At age six she started singing in church and became a gospel singer. Going to movies in the 1940s she would mimic scenes played by glamorous stars like **Bette Davis, Joan Crawford** and **Lena Horne**. In 1944 she began directing a young people's choir, and was often chosen to sing on the radio. That year, at age 13, she was hired to sing with **Mahalia Jackson**'s gospel group. She graduated high school at only 15, forming her own gospel group, Meditation Singers. She quit Wayne State University due to her mother's death and her father's illness to help support the family. After odd jobs, she started performing in clubs. She changed her name when she realized it was too long for the marquee.[152] Reese had one hit single, hosted a talk show, and starred on CBS's *Touched by an Angel*.

George Reeves (January 5, 1914 – June 16, 1959) American actor
Birth Name — George Keefer Brewer

1954, Superman, Public Domain

Born in Woodstock, Iowa, five months into the marriage of a couple who separated soon afterward, he moved with his mother to her home of Galesburg, Illinois. His mother later moved to California to live with her sister and married Frank Bessolo, while his father also remarried, never seeing his son again. George was adopted by Bessolo, but after 15 years his mother was divorced again, and his mother told George he had committed suicide. He began acting and singing in high school, then at Pasadena Junior College. He also boxed in amateur matches, but was ordered by his mother to stop. While acting at the Pasadena Playhouse he met his wife and got married. His career began in 1939 when he had a minor role in *Gone with the Wind*, but was incorrectly credited. He was soon contracted by Warner Brothers who changed his name to George Reeves.[153] He got a number of short roles before being drafted during World War II. In 1961 he almost turned down the starring TV role in The *Adventures of Superman* which was his crowning achievement.

Anne Rice (October 4, 1941-_____) American author of gothic fiction, Christian literature and erotica
Birth Name — Howard Allen O'Brien

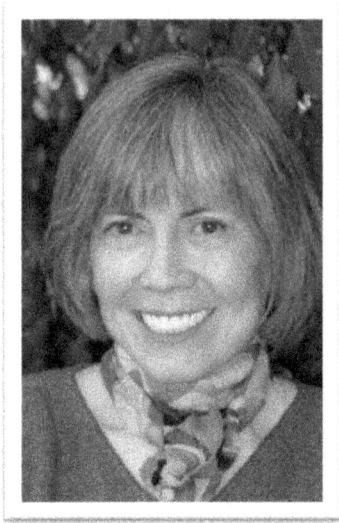

2006 Photo, Public Domain

Born in New Orleans to parents of Irish Catholic descent, Rice's father served in the Navy during World War II. She said that her unusual given name, Howard Allen was courtesy of her mother who thought that having a man's name would give her an unusual advantage in the world according to *You Asked, Anne Answered* on the Internet Archive *WayBack Machine*. Her authorized biography, *Prism in the Night* by **Katherine Ramsland**, page 10, however, gives her father as the culprit. She actually took the name Anne on the first day of school when a nun asked her name. She chose it because she thought it was a pretty name, and her mother never corrected it.[154] Her name was legally changed in 1947. Her mother died as a result of alcoholism at her age 15 and she and her sisters were placed in St. Joseph's Academy. The name Rice came from her husband, whom she met in a journalism class. She is best known for *The Vampire Chronicles* series of novels and their two film adaptations.

Little Richard (December 5, 1032-_____) American singer, songwriter and musician
Birth Name — Richard Wayne Penniman

1967 Photo, Public Domain

Born in Macon, Georgia, he was the third child of 12. His father was a church deacon who sold bootlegged moonshine on the side and owned a nightclub. He was nicknamed "**Lil' Richard**" by family members due to his skinny stature as a child.[155] He began singing in church as a child. Due to one leg being slightly shorter, he walked with a limp and was made fun of for allegedly looking effeminate. His highly religious family joined AME, Baptist and Pentecostal churches, some becoming ministers. Gifted with an especially high voice, Little Richard recalls that they were "always changing the key upwards." He sang so loud that he was called "War Hawk." His initial influences were gospel artists like **Brother Joe May, Mahalia Jackson** and **Sister Rosetta Tharp**, who was so impressed with his singing that she invited him to sing in her concert at his age 14. He first signed with Peacock Records, then after releasing *Tutti Frutti* on Specialty Records his career took off. Little Richard is a personal friend of a *St. Clair Publications* author who shall remain anonymous to protect her privacy.

159

Harold Robbins (May 21, 1916 – October 14, 1997) American author
Birth Name – Harold Rubin

1979, Netherlands, *Rob C. Croes/Anefo*
Creative Commons Attribution- Share Alike

Born in New York City to well-educated Russian and Polish Jewish immigrants, he was raised by his father and stepmother in Brooklyn. Dropping out of high school in the late 1920s he worked at a variety of jobs. He worked for Universal Pictures from 1940-'57, starting as a clerk and being promoted up to executive level.

Robbins first book, *Never Love a Stranger* (1958) was very controversial because of explicit sexuality. It was his publisher, **Alfred Komp**, who insisted on changing his name to Robbins.[156] Komp said it was because he thought it would look better on the book, but Harold thought that it was because Rubin was a recognizable Jewish name. He agreed, but refused to tone the book down by taking out some of the explicit language and sex scenes. Robbins is one of the best-selling authors of all times, with over 25 best-sellers including *The Carpetbaggers*, *A Stone for Danny* and *King Creole*, adapted for film, the latter starring **Elvis Presley**.

Ginger Rogers (July 16, 1911 – April 25, 1995) American dancer, singer and film star
Birth Name — Virginia Katherine McMath

1940s Publicity Photo, Public Domain

Born in Independence, Missouri, she was the only child of a Scottish electrical engineer father and Welsh mother which were separated before her birth. McMath kidnapped her twice, and afterward, Ginger never saw him again. While her mother went to Hollywood to get an essay she had written made into a film, she stayed with her grandparents. Successful in her venture, she continued to write scripts for Fox Studios. Rogers remained close to her grandfather and much later bought him a home in Sherman Oaks, California so he could be lose to her while she was filming. She got her stage name when one of her cousins had a hard name pronouncing Virginia and said "Ginga."[157] It stuck, being changed to Ginger. At her age nine, her mother remarried to John Logan Rogers, and she took his name though she was never legally adopted. Moving to Fort Worth, Texas, her mother became a theater critic for the *Fort Worth Record*. Though dreaming of teaching, her mother's influence began her career when a vaudeville act came to town. She became a stand in. On Broadway by 19, she soon got movie roles and paired with **Fred Aistaire**.

161

Roy Rogers (November 5, 1911 – July 6, 1998) American singer and cowboy actor "The King of the Cowboys"
Leonard Franklin Slye

1940, Public Domain

Leonard's family lived in a tenement building on the future site of Riverfront Stadium in Cincinnati, Ohio, where he was born. His dad and his brother built a houseboat from salvage lumber and in July, 1912, went up the River to Portsmouth and bought land to build a home. Due to the Great Flood of 1913 they moved the houseboat onto the land and lived in it. In 1919 they bought a farm at near Lucasville, Ohio. Taking a job in a shoe factory, Len's dad bought him a horse. He learned to ride, play mandolin, yodel and sing for square dances. Quitting school, Len went to work at the factory. His sister moved to California and the family followed. His sister made him a Western shirt and he went on a radio program. He was asked to sing with the **Western Mountaineers,** later hiring **Bob Nolan.** After that the **Sons of the Pioneers** came to be, recording *Tumbling Tumbleweed* and *Cool Water.* He was billed as Leonard Slye in his first film with **Gene Autry.** He first sang as Dick Weston, but when he was hired by Republic Pictures they changed his name to Roy Rogers.[158] He was one of the greatest cowboy stars ever.

Mickey Rooney (September 23, 1920 – April 6, 2014) American actor of film, television, radio and vaudeville, and comedian
Birth Name – Joseph Yule, Jr.

1940 Publicity Photo, Public Domain

Born in Brooklyn, New York, the only child of a Scottish-born father and American mother who were vaudeville performers, Rooney became a part of their show at age 15 to 17 months dressed in a tailored tux. While his father was traveling, he and his mother moved to her native Kansas City, Missouri to live with his aunt. His mom contacted **Hal Roach** to hire Joe, Jr. for the *Our Gang* series in Hollywood. He got only $5.00 per day while the others were paid $25.00. His first film role was in 1926. The next year he played in a series of short films as *Mickey McGuire*, taking the stage name Mickey Rooney.[159] He tried to change his name legally to *Mickey McGuire*, and began going by that name off screen, but because of a copyright suit, later settled, he stayed Rooney. He reached new heights in 1937 when he began playing Andy Hardy. He graduated high school in 1938 and played in *Boys Town*, and received an Oscar for the Andy Hardy role. Over almost nine decades he starred in more than 300 films.

Meg Ryan (November 19, 1961-_____) American actress and film producer

Birth Name – Margaret Mary Emily Anne Hyra

2010 Metropolitan Opera, *David Shankbone*, Creative Commons Attribution- Share Alike,

Meg was born in Fairfield, Connecticut to a math teacher father and former actress and English teacher mother. Her parents divorced at her age 15, and she attended Catholic elementary school, public high school, the University of Connecticut then New York University, acting in TV commercials and dropping out just prior to graduation, because she was already working successfully in acting.

Having gone by Peggy Hyra as a child, she decided that she preferred Meg as a shortened form of Margaret. When choosing a stage name she settled on her maternal grandmother's maiden name of Ryan.[160] Her film debut was in **George Cuker**'s *Rich and Famous;* then the role of Betsy Stewart on *As the World Turns* from 1982 to 1984. After other parts, she was cast opposite **Billy Crystal** in *When Harry Met Sally*, the first of several comedic hit movies including *Sleepless in Seattle* and *French Kiss*.

Winona Ryder (October 29, 1971-_____) American actress
Birth Name — Winona Laura Horowitz

2012 Press Conference, *Frankeweenie,*
Larry Richman, Creative Commons Attribution- Share Alike

Winona was born in Olmstead County, Minnesota to parents who were both authors and editors. Her father's family was Jewish from Romania and Russia, and many of them perished in the Holocaust. At her age seven, her family moved to a 300-acre commune in California where she became interested in acting when her mother showed her movies on a screen in the barn. In 1983 she enrolled in American Conservatory Theater and took acting lessons. In 1985 she auditioned for *Desert Bloom,* and though turned down, she was cast by Director **David Seltzer** in *Lucas,* 1986, filmed in summer '85 with **Charlie Sheen**. When asked how she wanted her name to appear in credits, she told them to use the surname Ryder because a **Mitch Ryder** album belonging to her father was playing in the background.[161] Her 1988 role in *Beetle Juice* won acclaim. *Mermaids* got her a Golden Globe nomination. Other roles followed including *Edward Scissorhands* (1990), and *Bram Stoker's Dracula* (1992). Then she won a Golden Globe and an Oscar nomination for Best Actress for her role in *The Age of Innocence* (1993).

Isla St. Clair (May 2, 1952-_____) Scottish singer, actress and former game show host
Birth Name — Isabella Margaret Dyce

Isla in 2004, Photo, *Melvin Sinclair, Jr.*

Isla was born in Grangemouth, central Scotland to a family from near Caithness, ancestral home of the Clan Sinclair for which I served for many years as a Commissioner, and as Eastern U.S. V.P. Her mother was songwriter and poet **Zetta Sinclair**. She gave her first performances at age three in Findochty, Moray, Scotland at her mother's concerts with the local Salvation Army. She then accompanied her mother to the Aberdeen Folk Club where they both sang. Coming to the attention of a BBC producer, at age twelve she sang on her first TV program, *Talk of the North*, followed by the radio series *Stories are for Singing*. Upon Zetta's remarriage in 1968, Isla adopted the original form of her mother's family name, St. Clair,[162] which my branch of the family bears. It was my great pleasure to meet Isla a few years ago at a Clan Gathering in Grandfather Mountain, North Carolina. She is a traditional country singer known by millions for her appearances on BBC's *Generation Game*.

Doctor Seuss (March 2, 1904 – September 24, 1991) American children's book writer and cartoonist

Birth Name — Theodore Seuss Geisel

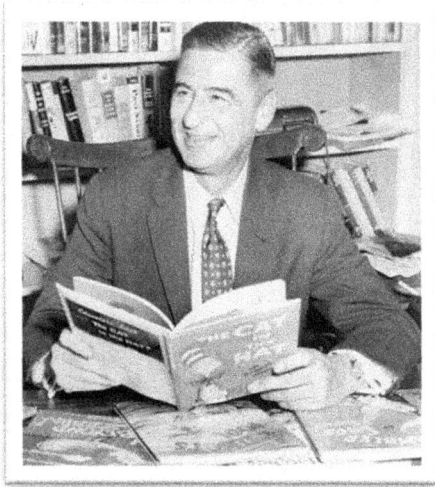

1957, *Al Ravenna*, Public Domain

Born in Springfield, Massachusetts, he was the grandson of German immigrants on both sides and raised Lutheran. He took art as a freshman in high school, graduating in 1921, afterward attending Dartmouth College, where he became editor-in-chief of humor magazine *Dartmouth Jack-O-Lantern*. When he was caught drinking gin with friends, he was asked to resign from the newspaper. In order to continue secretly, he began signing his work Seuss. Professor of rhetoric W. Benfield Pressey encouraged and inspired him. Graduating in 1925 he enrolled at Lincoln College, Oxford to work toward a PhD in English Literature. There he met Helen Palmer who encouraged him to pursue a drawing career. Without his degree, Geisel returned to Springfield and began submitting his work to magazines and publishers. His first nationally published cartoon appeared in *The Saturday Evening Post* on July 16, 1927, and he moved to New York. That year he was hired as a writer and illustrator for the humor magazine, *Judge,* and married Helen. Within 6 months he was publishing as **Dr. Seuss**.[163] There are 46 Dr. Seuss children's books.

Jane Seymour (February 15, 1951-_____) British-American actress
Birth Name — Joyce Penelope Wilhelmina Frankenberg

2009, Beverly Hills, *Ilya Haykinson,*
Creative Commons Attribution- Share Alike

Born in Middlesex, England, she was the daughter of a Polish-Jewish obstetrician father, a British citizen, and a nurse mother of Dutch protestant heritage, who was a POW during WW II and had lived in Indonesia. Joyce was educated in the Arts Educational School in Tring, Hertfordshire. At the onset of her acting career she intentionally chose the name of the third wife of King Henry VIII as her stage name.[164] In 1969 she appeared in **Richard Attenborough**'s *Oh! What a Lovely War.* Her first major film role was in 1970 as Lillian Stein, a Jewish woman seeking shelter from the Nazis in *The Only Way.* In 1973 she got her first major television series role in *The Onedin Line,* and numerous others followed. Then in 1980 she appeared with **Christopher Reeve** in the time travel romance *Somewhere in Time.* After others, in 1988 she was cast in mini-series *The Winds of War* and *War and Remembrance;* in the 1990's, *Dr. Quinn, Medicine Woman.* She has earned an Emmy and 3 Golden Globes.

168

Charlie Sheen (September 3, 1965-_____) American actor
Birth Name — Carlos Irwin Estavez

012 FX ad, *Jolla Marano,* Creative Commons Attribution- Share Alike

Born in New York City, he is the youngest son of actor **Martin Sheen,** and brother of actors **Emilio, Ramon** and **Renée Estevez.** The family moved to Malibu, California after Martin's Broadway turn in *The Subject was Roses.* Charlie's first film appearance was at age nine in his father's 1974 film, *The Execution of Private Slovik.* As a teen he made amateur Super 8 films with his brother Emilio and school friends **Rob Lowe** and **Sean Penn.** Just before graduation he was expelled from high school for poor grades and attendance and decided on a career in acting, taking the stage name Sheen, [165] with the first name Charlie. His father had taken the name in honor of **Bishop Fulton Sheen.**[166] His first role was in 1984 in *Red Dawn* with *Patrick Swayze,* **C. Thomas Howell, Lea Thompson,** and **Jennifer Grey.** Then he and Grey were paired again in *Ferris Bueller's Day Off* in 1986. Other notable films included *Platoon* (1986), *Wall Street* (1988), *Young Guns* (1988), *Born on the Fourth of July* (1989), and comedy roles *in Major League* (1989) and *Hot Shots* (1991).

Martin Sheen (August 3, 1940-_____) American actor
Birth Name — Ramon Antonio Gerardo

2009, *Brian Mc Guirk*, C. C. Att.- Share Alike

Born in Dayton, Ohio to a Spanish immigrant father and Irish immigrant mother, Sheen's left arm was crushed at birth with forceps causing limited use of it. Drawn to acting young, he borrowed money from a Catholic priest and moved to New York City in his early 20s to pursue acting. Spending two years in the Living Theater Company he met Catholic Activist **Dorothy Day** and worked with her Catholic Worker Movement for social justice. He later played movement co-founder **Peter Maurin** in *Entertaining Angels: The Dorothy Day Story*. He took his stage name from CBS casting director, **Robert Dale Martin** and **Bishop Fulton J. Sheen**.[165] When asked by *Stargazer Magazine* why he changed his name Sheen said, "I never changed it officially. I never will. It's on my driver's license and passport and everything: Ramon Gerard Estevez. I started using Sheen, I thought I'd give it a try, and before I knew it, I started making a living with it and then it was too late. In fact, one of my great regrets is that I didn't keep my name as it was given to me. I knew it bothered my dad."[166] He achieved fame from *Badlands* (1973) and *Apocalypse Now* (1979). On NBC's *West Wing* he played a President.

170

Sidney Sheldon (February 11, 1917 – January 30, 2007) American writer

Birth Name — Sidney Schechtel

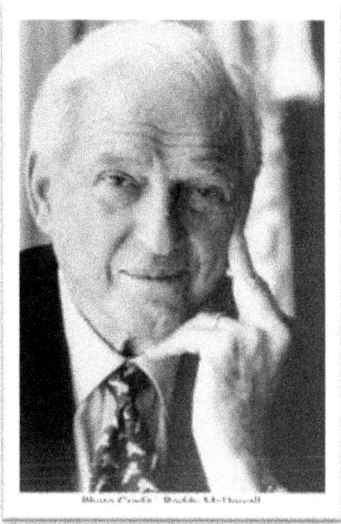

1970, *Roddy McDowell*, Public Domain

Sheldon was born in Chicago to parents of Russian Jewish ancestry. His father was a jewelry store manager. After graduating from high school he attended Northwestern University and wrote short plays for drama groups. He was forced to drop out during the Great Depression working at a variety of jobs. One of his jobs, as a radio announcer, prompted him to change his last name to Sheldon.[167] In 1937 he moved to Hollywood where he reviewed film scripts, working on several B movies. In World War II he became a pilot on the Army Air Corps, but his band disbanded before he could see action. After that he moved to New York and started writing musical plays for Broadway, continuing to work on screenplays. His success on Broadway took him back to Hollywood. His first assignment, The *Bachelor and the Bobby-Soxer* earned him an Academy Award for Best Screenplay in 1947. First producing *The Patty Duke Show*, he created, produced and wrote *I Dream of Jennie, Hart to Hart*, and many other shows. From 1969, he became a best-selling author.

Dinah Shore (February 29, 1916 – February 24, 1994) American singer, actress and television personality
Birth Name — Frances Rose Shore

1951 Publicity Photo, Public Domain

Born in Winchester, Tennessee, Shore was stricken with polio at age two, and walked with a limp, a feature which made her shy. Later moving briefly at age eight to my home town of McMinnville, Tennessee, then to Nashville, where in spite of her limp she became active in cheerleading in high school at age 14. She debuted as a torch singer at a night club that year without her parents' consent. They allowed the singing there, but forced her to put a career in music on hold. After her mother's unexpected demise, Shore attended Vanderbilt University, ultimately obtaining a degree in sociology. During college she went to the Grand Ole Opry and made her debut on WSM radio which aired the show. She then went to New York to audition for orchestras and radio stations while on summer break from Vanderbilt, and after graduation in 1936 she moved there. In a number of her auditions she sang the popular song *Dinah*. When DJ **Martin Brock** forgot her name he called her "Dinah Girl," and the name stuck, so she adapted it as her stage name.[168] She became a top female artist of the 1940s and in the 1950s hosted a TV show sponsored by Chevrolet for which she sang the theme, *See the U.S.A. in your Chevrolet*, which became her signature song.

Gene Simmons (August 25, 1949-_____) Israeli-American bass guitarist, singer-songwriter, record producer, actor, TV personality
Birth Name — Chaim Witz

2012, Los Angeles © *Glenn Francis*
www.ProDigital.com , Creative Commons- Share Alike

Born in Haifa, Israel, he immigrated with his Hungarian born, Holocaust survivor mother, Flora Klein to Queens, New York at age 8, while his father remained in Israel. Klein has the Hungarian equivalent *Kis*, but this is not the source of the band's name. Adopting his mother's maiden name, he became part of a Jewish sect community in Williamsburg, Brooklyn as a child. In the late '60s he changed his name to Gene Simmons to honor rockabilly singer **Jumpin' Gene Simmons**.[169] He was moved by the **Beatles** appearance on the *Ed Sullivan Show*, and became involved with his first band, *Lynx,* renamed *The Missing Links*, as a teen and later formed The Long Island Sounds. After attending community college he joined a band called Bullfrog Bheer and recorded a demo of "*Leeta*," later included in a *Kiss* box set. Forming the band Wicked Lester with **Paul Stanley**, they walked away from a deal with Epic Records to form **Kiss** with **Peter Criss** and **Ace Frehley**. He is a big fan of sci-fi comics, and his eye makeup came from a comic book picture.

Anne Sinclair (July 15, 1948-_____) American-born French Jewish television and radio personality/political show host
Birth Name — Anne-Elise Schwartz

Anne Sinclair

Anne was born in New York to French-born Jewish parents who fled France from Nazi persecution in 1940. Her maternal grandfather, Paul Rosenberg, was one of France's, later New York's, biggest art dealers. While young, her family returned to France and she attended the Cours Hattemer; then majored in politics at Paris Institute of Political Studies and in law at the University of Paris. Her father, Joseph-Robert Schwartz, changed his name to Sinclair in 1949.[170] Her first radio hosting job was at Europe 1. From 1985 to '87 she hosted a Sunday evening news political show, TF1, on television, becoming one of the country's best known journalists during its 13-year run. She interviewed **Bill Clinton, Mikhail Gorbachev** and even **Prince Charles**. But she also had celebrity guests like **Sharon Stone, Paul McCartney** and **Woody Allen**. Sinclair won 3 *Sept d'Or*, French equivalent of the Emmy Awards. Anne received even more wide notoriety as the wife of **Dominique Strauss-Kahn** when he was accused of rape in New York in 2012, after which they divorced.

Nikki Sixx (December 11, 1958-_____) American musician, songwriter, radio host and photographer
Birth Name — Frank Carlton Ferrana, Jr.

2007, Bryant Park, NYC,
Photo by *Christopher Peterson*, christopherpeterson.com (notified)

Born in San Jose, California, Sixx was raised by his single mother and his grandparents after his mother left. His mother's sister's husband, **Don Zimmerman**, is the president of Capitol Records. While living in Idaho as a teen Nikki turned to selling drugs and vandalism. After being sent by his grandparents to Seattle to live with his mother, he learned to play bass guitar which he had bought with money from a guitar he had stolen. At 17, he moved to Los Angeles and worked various jobs, and auditioned for bands, joining the group **Sister** led by **Blackie Lawless**. During that time he legally changed his name to Nikki Sixx.[171] He recorded a demo and along with **Lizzie Grey** was fired from the band. They formed **London** in 1978. In 1981 he founded **Mötley Crüe** with drummer **Tommy Lee**, guitarist **Mick Mars** and **Vince Neal**. Their debut album, *Too Fast for Love* was re-released later on Elektra Records; then *Shout for the Devil* became a national hit. *Dr. Feelgood* sold even more.

Anna Nicole Smith (November 28, 1967 – February 8, 2007)
Birth Name — Vickie Lynn Hogan

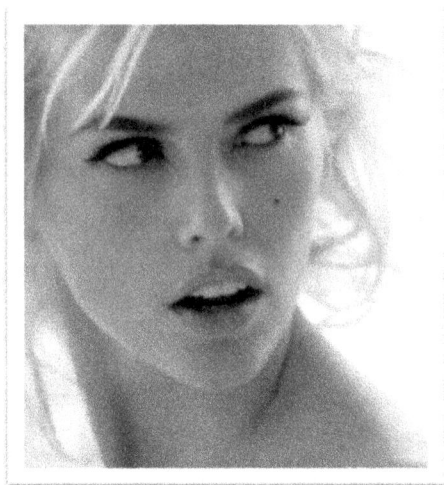

Pinterest, Public Domain

Born in Houston, Texas, her parents were married less than three years. After her mother remarried to Donald Hart, she changed her name to Nikki Hart. When she was in the 9th grade she was sent to live with her mother's younger sister, Key Beal in Mexia, Texas, where she failed her freshman year and dropped out in her sophomore year. While working at Jim's Krispy Fried Chicken she married Billy Smith, a cook there, at her age 17. In early 1992, she went to a photo shoot for *Playboy Magazine*. **Hugh Hefner** was so impressed he insisted that she be on the cover of the March issue. She was photographed in a low cut black evening gown and listed as Vickie Smith. The centerfold was shot by **Stephen Wayda**. The issue made her an overnight modeling sensation. At that time she settled on the name Anna Nicole Smith and aspired to be the next **Marilyn Monroe**.[172] Right away she was contracted by Guess Jeans, who saw a resemblance to **Jayne Mansfield** and photographed her in several sessions inspired by her. She appeared on the covers of several other major magazines and had a film and television career, but her son's death, drug addiction and personal woes led to her early demise.

176

Suzanne Somers (October 16, 1946-_____) American actor, author, singer, businesswoman and healthcare spokesperson
Birth Name — Suzanne Marie Mahoney

2005, USO, *Lameer Witter*, Public Domain

Born in San Bruno, California, Suzanne was the 3rd of 4 children born to an Irish-American Catholic family. Her father was an abusive alcoholic, and she feared for her life. In high school she was active in theater. She attended San Francisco College for Women, but got pregnant after 6 months and married the baby's father, **Bruce Somers** in '65.[173] Unhappy in the marriage, she had an affair and her husband divorced her. She was a prize model on a game show (1969-'70) where she got pregnant again by married host **Alan Hamel**. She had an abortion but later married him. She began acting small roles in the late 1960s and early '70s, keeping her son's name Somers, and appeared as a guest star on *Six Million Dollar Man* in 1977, soon landing her career-defining role as Chrissy Snow on *Three's Company*, which ended in a pay dispute in the 5th season. She did a nude shoot for *Playboy* in the '70s, later denying it; then the pictures were published in 1980 and '84. During the '80s, she had a show at the Los Vegas Hilton, which I saw. In 2012 she starred in her own Lifetime Network show; then she was a 2015 contestant on *Dancing with the Stars*.

Joe South (February 28, 1940 – September 5, 2012) American singer, songwriter and guitarist

Birth Name—Joseph Alfred Souter

1970 **Publicity Shot**, Pub. Dom.

While living in Atlanta in the late 1960s and early '70s, I became close friends with, a kind gentleman considerably older than I was. His name was Frank Souter and he was Joe's father's brother. It was at the time of Joe's greatest popularity and I loved his music. Uncle Frank, as we called him, told me that Joe and his brother, Tommy, who played drums, changed their last name to South because they liked the sound of it.[174] Joe began his pop music career in July, 1958, with the release *The Purple People Eater Meets the Witch Doctor* on NRC Records, but later songs were much more serious. He wrote songs recorded by many other great artists. Joe won a Grammy for *Games People Play* in 1970, and was nominated again in '72 for *Rose Garden* recorded by **Lynn Anderson**. South also wrote songs recorded by **Jerry Lee Lewis, Johnny Cash, Glen Campbell, Carol Burnett, Andy Williams, Dottie West** and many more, and was inducted into the Songwriter's Hall of Fame in 1976. I felt a personal loss at his death, and did a lengthy blog entry on him.

Dusty Springfield (April 16, 1939 –March 2, 1999) English pop singer and record producer
Birth Name — Mary Isobel Catherine O'Brien

1966, Public Domain

Born in West Hampstead, London, England, she was the 2nd child of Irish ancestry parents. Her father was raised in British India and worked as a tax accountant, while her mother's family was from Kerry, Ireland. Raised in Buckinghamshire and West London, Mary attended an all-girl Convent School. She was given the nickname "Dusty" for playing football with boys in the street and being a tomboy. But the family loved music. She listened to music by **Cole Porter, Count Basie, Rogers and Hammerstein** and others, but admired **Peggy Lee** and **Jo Stafford**, and wanted to sing like them. At age 12 she made a recording singing an **Irving Berlin** song in Ealing. She and her brother, Tom, began singing at local clubs. She then joined the **Lana Sisters**, harmonizing and performing on TV. In 1960 she formed the **Springfields**, she and Tom and **Mike Hurst** changing their names to Springfield,[175] going to Nashville, Tennessee to record an album. In 1963 they recorded UK top hit *Say I Won't Be There;* then she began her solo career with *I Only Want to Be With You,* her style altered to R&B. She had 6 top 20 hits in the U.S.

179

Cat Stevens/Yusef Islam (July 21, 1948-_____) English singer, songwriter, instrumentalist, humanitarian and philanthropist
Birth Name — Steven Demetre Georgiou

1970's Publicity Photo, Public Domain

Born in the Marylebone section of London, he was the 3ʳᵈ child of a Greek father and Swedish mother. The family lived above a restaurant, which his parents ran, and in which all of the family worked. At about his age 8 his parents divorced, but continued to live and work together. The family had a baby grand piano, but no one played well, so he taught himself. Inspired by the **Beatles**, he begged his father to buy him a guitar at 15 and began playing it and writing songs. Living near Denmark Street, the center of music, he listened on the rooftop. Interested in art and music, he and his mom moved to Sweden where he learned from a painter uncle; then returned to England and enrolled at Hammersmith School of Art. Determined to be a songwriter, in 1965 he signed a publishing deal and made demos. He began to perform in coffee houses and pubs, and impressed **Mike Hurst**, formerly of the **Springfields,** getting a record deal under the stage name Cat Stevens, because a girlfriend said he had "eyes like a cat."[176] Later converting to Islam, he changed his name again in '77, to Yusef Islam to work for Mohammed.[177]

Jon Stewart (November 28, 1962-_____) American comedian, writer, producer, actor, media critic and television host
Birth Name — Jonathan Stuart Leibowitz

2008, USO Metro Awards, Pub. Dom.

Born the second of four sons in New York City to Litvak Jewish parents whose families emigrated from Poland, Ukraine and Belarus, his father was a professor of physics at two colleges and his mother was a teacher and educational consultant. After his parents divorced at his age 11, he was mostly estranged from his father.

Jon graduated from The College of William and Mary, which I recently visited at Williamsburg, Virginia, in 1984, majoring in psychology. After college he returned to the New York City metro where he worked the comedy club circuit, and held various jobs. He made his stand-up debut in The Bitter End where his idol, **Woody Allen** started. Because of this strained relationship, Jon dropped his surname and started using his middle name. He had his name legally changed to the alternate spelling of Stewart in 2001.[178] He is best known for hosting *The Jon Stewart Show* on MTV and *The Daily Show* on Comedy Central which won 18 Emmys.

Donna Summer (December 31, 1948 – May 17, 2012) American singer, songwriter and painter "The Queen of Disco"
Birth Name — LaDonna Adrian Gaines

1979 Publicity Photo, Public Domain

Born in Boston, Massachusetts, Donna was one of 7 children of a butcher father and school teacher mother. At age 8 she first sang a solo in church, replacing a vocalist who failed to show. In high school she was popular for performances in school musicals and left before graduation to join the blues-rock band **Crow** in New York. After the band's breakup, she was accepted for a role in the musical, *Hair,* moving to Munich, Germany for production. She became fluent in German, performing in other plays. Within 3 years she moved to Vienna, Austria. In 1968 she released her first single as Donna Gaines in Germany, the second in 1971 on the European division of Decca Records, and in '72, *If You Walkin' Alone* on Philips Records. In 1973 she married Austrian actor **Helmuth Sommer**, having their daughter the same year. There she met producers **Giorgio Moroder** and **Pete Bellotte** during a recording session. After signing to Oasis label in 1974, they made an error on the record cover, listing her name as Donna Summer, and the name stuck.[179] She had four *Billboard* number one singles in the U.S. in 12 months and won five Grammys.

Mother Teresa (26 August 1910 – 5 September 1997) Albanian-Macedonian born Roman Catholic nun, missionary aka Teresa of Calcutta
Birth Name – Agnes Gonxha Bojaxhiu

1980s, Public Domain Image

She was born in Skopje in the Ottoman Empire, where her family lived until moving to Tirana, Albania in 1934. She was the youngest of an Albanian politician father. According to a biography by **Joan Graff Clucas**, she was inspired in youth by stories of missionaries in Bengal. She committed to a life of spiritual dedication taking a pledge on 15 August 1928 while praying at the shrine of the Black Madonna of Letnice. At 18 she left to join the Sisters of Loreto as a missionary, never seeing her mother or sister again. She went to their Abby in Ireland to learn English; then to India in 1929, beginning her novitiate in Darjeeling, near the Himalayas. She learned Bengali and taught at the St. Teresa School, taking first vows on 24 May 1931. There she chose to be named after **Thérèse de Lisieux**, patron saint of missionaries. A nun there already used that name so she chose the Spanish spelling of Teresa.[180] She took her final solemn vows on 14 May 1937. She formed the Missionaries of Charity, with over 4,500 sisters in 133 countries.

Akon (Thiam) (April 16, 1973-_____) American R&B and hip hop recording artist, songwriter, businessman , and record producer
Birth Name — Aliaune Damala Bouga Time Bongo Puru Nacka Lu Lu Lu Badara Akon Thiam

2008, Akon, *Va.sc*, Creative Com- Share Alike

Though he was born in St. Louis, Missouri, much of his childhood was spent in Senegal in West Africa, his family's homeland. His father was a percussionist and Akon learned to play 5 instruments while growing up in Africa and Newark, New Jersey. He had trouble coping with his peers in Newark while his father moved to Atlanta, Georgia. He spent three years in jail during which he developed even more appreciation for music. Rapper **Lif Zane** took him along to **Devyane Stevens** Upfront Megatainment rehearsal hall and Stevens became Akon's mentor. Later Akon lost a deal with Elektra Records and Stevens brought him to the attention of Universal's SRC Records. His recording of *Lonely* struck **Jerome Foster** as a "huge record," and he hopped on a plane and flew to Atlanta to meet Akon. Usually credited as merely Akon, he sometimes uses his true last name, but always used Akon rather than his first name, Aliaune,[181] for obvious reasons of simplicity. It has been questioned whether Akon is actually even a part of his name, since his full name has also been reported as Aliaune Badara Thiam. He rose to fame in 2004 with the release of his single "*Locked Up*" from debut album, *Trouble*.

184

Michael "Mike" Todd (June 22, 1909-March 22, 1958) American theater and film producer
Birth Name — Avrom Hirsch Goldbogen

1956 Publicity Photo, Public Domain

Born in Minneapolis, Minnesota, Todd was the son of Polish Jewish immigrants; his father, an Orthodox rabbi. The youngest son of 9 siblings in a poor family, he was nicknamed Toat to mimic his attempt at pronouncing coat. From this, his stage name derived.[182] They moved into Chicago on the day World War I ended. He was expelled from the 6th grade for running craps game. In high school he produced the play *The Mikado.* Later he and a brother opened a construction company which contracted for Hollywood soundproofing production stages during transition to sound films. After failure during the depression, Todd produced an attraction called the "Flame Dance" in Chicago in 1933, getting a New York Casino offer. In 1939 he produced a jazz musical version of *The Mikado* for Broadway starring Bill "**Bo Jangles**" Robinson. He ultimately produced 17 Broadway shows. In 1950 he formed Cinerama with **Lowell Thomas** and **Fred Waller**, with a widescreen process he used to produce *Around the World in 80 Days.* His 3rd marriage was to **Elizabeth Taylor,** but he lived just over a year afterward.

Rip Torn (February 6, 1931-_____) American actor, voice artist and comedian
Birth Name — Elmore Rual Torn

1994 Emmys, *Alan Light*, Creative Commons Attribution

Born in Elmore, Texas, Torn's father was an agriculturist and economist. Bring given the nickname Rip is a tradition in the Torn family for several generations, and his father, also called Rip, passed it on to him.[183] He attended Texas A&M, majoring in animal husbandry, then hitchhiked to Hollywood, hoping to become a movie star. His goal was to save money to buy a ranch. Working various jobs, he got occasional TV roles, but his feature film debut was a small part in **Eliza Kazan**'s *Baby Doll* in 1956. Moving to New York City, he studied under **Lee Strasburg** at the Actors' Studio, also studying dance under **Martha Graham**. Between 1957 and 1960 he appeared regularly in live shows like *Omnibus* and *Playhouse 90*. He made his Broadway debut in *Sweet Bird of Youth* on March 10, 1959, winning a Tony in 1960 for Best Supporting Actor in a play, as well as a Theater Award. Torn earned a great reputation as an actor in plays, films and television, winning an Oscar, six Emmys and other awards.

186

Randy Travis (May 4, 1959-_____) American singer, songwriter, guitarist and actor

Birth Name – Randy Bruce Traywick

2013, Nashville, *Larry Philpot* of SundstagePhotography.com, Creative Commons Attribution-Share Alike

Born in Marshville, North Carolina, Randy's father was a farmer, and owner of a construction business; his mother, a textile worker. His father was a fan of **Hank Williams** and other country stars of his day and encouraged sons Randy and Ricky to pursue country music. At age 8 Randy was playing guitar and singing in church. Two years later he and Ricky began performing as the Traywick Brothers. Randy dropped out of school and became a juvenile delinquent. In 1975 Randy won a talent contest at a night club in Charlotte. The club's owner, **Lib Hatcher**, took an interest in him, becoming his manager. In 1978 he recorded an album using his birth name. Hatcher left her husband after Randy moved in with her. After he was rejected by major labels, Hatcher went to work managing The Nashville Palace and recorded him live performing there to get him a record deal with Warner Brothers, who named him Randy Travis.[184] He has sold over 25,000,000 albums and won 33 major awards.

Tina Turner (November 26, 1939-_____) American singer, dancer, actress and author

Birth Name — Anna Mae Bullock

1985, Drammenshallen, Norway, *Helge Øverås*, Creative Commons Attribution- Share Alike

Turner was born near Nutbush, Tennessee, where her father oversaw sharecroppers. During World War II Anna stayed with her strict paternal grandparents. After the war returning to Nutbush, Anna sang in the church choir. Her mother left her abusive father, moving to St. Louis, Missouri, and he remarried, going to Detroit. She went to live with her grandmother in Brownsville, who died suddenly and she went live with her mother. There at Club Manhattan she first saw **Ike Turner**. Longing to sing with him, at 18, one night the drummer gave her the mic during intermission. Ike asked her to join them. Her first tape was in the name Little Ann. In 1960, Ike wrote *A Fool in Love* for Art Lassiter who failed to show. Anna recorded it and sent it to **Juggy Murray** of Sue Records who was impressed and bought the track for $25,000, telling Ike to make her the star of his show. Then he changed her name to Tina.[185] It was a smash hit. Ike and Tina were married from November 26, 1962 to March 29, 1978. She has sold more than 100 million records, winning 8 Grammys.

Mark Twain (November 30, 1835 – April 21, 1910) American author and humorist
Birth Name — Samuel Langhorn Clemmons

1871 Portrait, *Matthew Brady,* Public Domain

The sixth son of seven children born to a Virginian father and mother from Kentucky, Clemmons was born in Florida, Missouri, and reared in Hannibal, a port town on the Mississippi River, which supplied the fictional setting for the *Adventures of Huckleberry Finn* and *Tom Sawyer.* Only 3 siblings survived childhood. When he was 11, in 1847, his father, an attorney and judge, died of pneumonia, and Sam quit school after the 10th grade to become a printer's apprentice. 4 years later he began type-setting then submitting articles and humorous tales to the *Hannibal Journal.* At 18 he left to work as a printer in New York, Philadelphia, St. Louis and Cincinnati. Joining the printer's union, he educated himself in libraries. Horace Bixby, a steamboat pilot, took him on as a cub pilot to teach him the river between St. Louis and New Orleans for $500, to be paid out of his wages. Over 2 years later he got his pilot's license. From piloting he took his pen name Mark Twain, the cry for a depth of over two fathoms.[186] He was called the Father of American Literature. *The Adventures of Tom Sawyer* is available from *St. Clair Publications Classics.*

189

Shania Twain (August 28, 1965-_____) Canadian singer and songwriter

Birth Name — Eileen Regina Edwards

2011 Juneau Awards, Toronto, *Sara Collaton*,CC

Born in Windsor, Ontario, her parents divorced at her age 2 and her mother married Jerry Twain, an Ojibwa who adopted her 2 girls. Struggling financially, Shania started singing in bars at age 8 to help pay bills. Though she hated this at the time, it helped her survive, and she began writing songs at age 10. At 13 she to performed on CBC TV's *The Tommy Hunter Show*. In high school she sung with a local band, Longshot. Then she took singing lessons from **Ian Garrett**. In fall of '84 **Stan Campbell** with *Country Music News* noticed her, took her to Nashville to do demos and she met country singer **Mary Bailey** who moved her into her home and introduced her to **John Bell**, whom she began dating. Wanting to do rock, she fell out with Bailey in 2 years. She changed her name in '91 to Shania, a Native Ojibwa word meaning On My Way.[187] In 1993 she did a self-titled country album on Mercury Records which was certified platinum. She reached super-stardom after meeting **Mutt Lange** who co-wrote, managed and married her. She is one of the world's best selling artists of all time, winning 5 Grammys.

Conway Twitty (September 1, 1933 – June 5, 1993) American singer and musician
Birth Name — Harold Jenkins

1974 Publicity Photo, Public Domain

Born in Coahoma County, Mississippi, he was named by his great uncle after his favorite silent movie star, Harold Lloyd. The family moved to Helena, Arkansas at his age 10. There Harold started his own singing group, the Phillips County Ramblers. Within two years he had his own local radio show each Saturday morning. Baseball was also a passion and after high school he got an offer to play for the Philadelphia Phillies, but was drafted into the Army where he organized a group to entertain the troops. A neighbor encouraged him to pursue music as a career, and after hearing **Elvis Presley's** *Mystery Train* he began writing rock music. He went to Sun Records in Memphis and worked with **Sam Phillips** to get the right sound. In 1957 he decided that he needed a stage name, and though accounts vary, **Fred Bronson** in *The Billboard Book of Number One Hits* says that on a map he spotted Conway, Arkansas and Twitty, Texas and chose the name Conway Twitty.[188] He had success crossing genres of country, rock, R&B and pop and held the record for most number one singles on *Billboard Country Hits* until 2006.

191

Rudolph Valentino (May 6, 1895 – August 23, 1926) Italian-born American silent film actor
Birth Name — Rodolpho Alfonso Raffaello Pierre Filibert Guglielmi di Valentina d'Antonguolla

1923 Publicity Photo, Public Domain

An early pop icon and sex symbol of the 1920s, he was known as the Latin Lover or simply Valentino. The name was a shortening of his complex birth name.[189] After losing his sister to death, he was petted by his mother, and was spoiled and troublesome, but eventually earned a degree in Genoa in spite of problems in school. After a brief stint in Paris, he returned to Italy but was unable to find work and traveled to New York, being processed at Ellis Island at age 18.

He befriended a married heiress with whom he reportedly had an affair. After her divorce, her ex-husband had Valentino arrested on vice charges. The heiress then shot her ex-husband over a custody dispute. Valentino left with a traveling musical to the West, joining a production of *Robinson Crusoe, Jr.* in Los Angeles. That fall in San Francisco he met **Norman Kerry** who got him into silent films. He was a huge hit but died at age 31. He starred a lot with **Nadia Nildi** (also featured).

Frankie Valli (May 3, 1934-_____) American popular singer
Birth Name — Francesco Stephen Castelluccio

1970s Show Photo, Public Domain

Born the third and final child of Italian parents in Newark, his dad was a barber and Lionel train display designer, while his mom worked for a beer company. His mother took him to see **Frank Sinatra** at age 7, and he was inspired to be a singer. He took his stage name from his early mentor, **"Texas" Jean Valli**.[190] He worked as a barber until he could support himself as a singer. He began singing professionally in 1951 in the **Variety Trio** with **Tommy DeVito** and **Nick Macioci**. He recorded his first single, *My Mother's Eyes*, in 1953 as Frankie Valley. He and DeVito then formed **The Variatones** with **Hank Majewski, Frank Cattone** and **Billy Thompson**. In '56 they backed a female singer and impressed **Peter Paul**, who auditioned them for RCA Victor the next week. Renamed **The Four Lovers**, they recorded several singles and an album track. DeVito and Majewski left and were replaced by **Nick Macioci** (now Massi) and **Hugh Garity.** In '59 **Bob Gaudio** joined, and after more changes, **The Four Seasons** were born. In 1962, *Sherry* and *Big Girls Don't Cry* began a long string of hits for this popular group.

193

Abigail Van Buren (July 4, 1918 – January 16, 2013) American nationally syndicated advice columnist and radio host
Birth Name — Pauline Ester Friedman

1961 Publicity Photo, Public Domain

Nicknamed "Popo" by her family, "Abby" was born in Sioux City, Iowa to Russian Jewish immigrants who had nothing and ended up owning a chain of movie theaters. She had an identical twin with a near-identical name, Esther Pauline. They ended up with near-identical lives. Both went to Morningside College where both studied journalism and psychology, writing a joint gossip column for the college newspaper. In 1939 they were both married in a double ring ceremony on their 21st birthday. New to the area, in January, 1956, she phoned "Auk" Arnold, editor of the *San Francisco Chronicle* and said that she could write a better advice column than the one in the paper. He gave her some letters and told her to bring back her answers in a week. When she brought them back an hour and a half later she was hired. She got her pen name from the biblical book of Samuel: *Then David said to Abigail ... 'Blessed is your advice and blessed are you.'* Van Buren was from the president, **Martin Van Buren.**[191] Her column, *Dear Abby*, was the most widely syndicated advice column in the world. Her twin sister became columnist **Ann Landers**.

Bobby Vee (April 30, 1943- _____) American pop singer/teen idol

Birth Name — Robert Thomas Velline

Circa 1962, Public Domain

Bobby was born in Fargo, North Dakota, and on February 3, 1959, at the age of 15, when **Buddy Holly, Richie Valens** and the **Big Bopper** (all featured in this book) were killed en route to do a show in Morehead, Minnesota, Velline hastily assembled a band of schoolboys of Fargo calling themselves **The Shadows** to fill in for Holly and crew. Their performance was a success setting in motion the beginning of his career. That year he took the stage name Bobby Vee[192] and released his first single, an original song, *Suzie Baby* on Soma Records patterned after Holly's *Peggy Sue*. It was a regional hit. That year he hired a pianist from Hibbing who said his name was Elston Gunn to play back up with **The Shadows.** He would later become more famous than Vee as **Bob Dylan.**

In 1960, his next single, *Rubber Ball*, on Liberty Records, made him a national star. Other hits included *Take Good Care of my Baby, Run to Him* and *The Night Has a Thousand Eyes*. He charted 10 in the top 20 pop hits.

John Wayne (May 26, 1907 – June 11, 1979) American film actor and producer
Birth Name — Marion Robert Morrison

1965 Publicity Photo, Public Domain

Born at home in Winterset, Iowa, he was of Scottish heritage and brought up Presbyterian. The family moved to Glendale, California where a local fireman started calling him "Little Duke" because he took his Airedale Terrier, Duke, everywhere. As a teen he worked in an ice cream shop for a man who shod horses for Hollywood studios and played football at Glendale High School. Being turned down by the Naval Academy, he attended the University of Southern California, on a football scholarship. An injury caused him to lose that, so he was forced to drop out of college. As a favor to coach **Howard Jones** who had given **Tom Mix** USC football tickets, **John Ford** and Mix hired Wayne as a prop boy and extra. There he became friends with **Wyatt Earp** and got bit parts for Fox Films. After uncredited roles, he was given the name Duke Morrison in *Words and Music* (1929). Director **Raul Walsh** cast him in *The Big Trail* (1930) and suggested stage name Anthony Wayne after a Revolutionary war hero. Rejected by the studio, he changed it to John Wayne.[193] In the top box-office draws for three decades, he epitomized rugged masculinity.

Tuesday Weld (August 27, 1943-_____) American actress
Birth Name—Susan Ker Weld

Circa 1960 Publicity, Public Domain

Born in New York City, her father died just before her 4th birthday. Her mother, Yosene Balfour Ker, was the daughter of the artist and *Life* illustrator **William Balfour Ker**. Financially strapped after her husband's death, her mother put Susan to work as a model as a young child. When she was 12, she secured an agent who needed a stage name for her. Her young cousin, Mary, couldn't pronounce Susan and called her Tu-tu, so the name Tuesday was born from this[194] when she made her acting debut on TV. Soon she got a bit part in **Alfred Hitchcock**'s 1956 crime drama, *The Wrong Man*. Weld was so pressured that she had a nervous breakdown at age nine; alcoholism and a suicide attempt at age 12. In 1956 at 13, she played the lead in the movie *Rock, Rock, Rock* with **Alan Freed, Chick Berry, Chuck Lymon** and **Johnny Burnette**. But **Connie Francis** did the vocals on Weld's singing parts. In 1959, after another film part, she was cast as Thalia Menninger in the CBS series, *The Many Loves of Dobie Gillis,* creating publicity for her, winning her a Golden Globe for Most Promising Newcomer. Under 20th Century Fox contract she made many films and TV shows. She won an Emmy in 1983; a BFTA in '84.

Dottie West (October 11, 1932 – September 4, 1991) American country music singer and songwriter
Birth Name — Dorothy Marie Marsh

Circa 1965 Publicity Shot, Public Dom.

Dottie's signature song, also used in a commercial for Coca Cola, says, "*I was Raised on Country Sunshine.*" She surely was. She was born and raised in my hometown for the past thirty-eight years, McMinnville, Tennessee, where her mother ran a restaurant. One of her nieces was the first wife of one of my wife's brothers, so our nephews are her great nephews. But her father was abusive and was sentenced to 40 years in prison. Dottie got a music scholarship to Tennessee Tech in Cookeville, where she met her first husband, musician Bill West, whose name she took and kept.[195]

Dottie was one of country music's most influential and groundbreaking female artists. Her 1964 hit, *Here Comes My Baby Back Again* won her in 1965 the first ever Grammy of its type for *Best Female Country Vocal Performance*. She was a profound influence on artists like **Lynn Anderson, Barbara Mandrell, Dolly Parton** and **Tammy Wynette**. In the late '70s she and **Kenny Rogers** recorded several duets, which helped her reach her peak of popularity, leading to her first solo number one song in 1980, *A Lesson in Leavin'*. She was killed in an auto accident on the way to a Grand Ole Opry performance for which she was late.

Mae West (August 17, 1893 – November 22, 1980) American actress, singer, playwright, screenwriter and sex symbol

Birth Name – Mary Jane West

1932 Movie Photo, Public Domain

West was born at home in Brooklyn, New York, delivered by a midwife. Her father was a prizefighter and her mother a Bavarian immigrant who had worked as a corset model. At age five, she first entertained at a church social and at seven started appearing in amateur shows, often winning. She began performing in vaudeville at 14 using the stage name Baby Mae. Trying different personas, she used techniques from both male and female impersonators. Her first Broadway performance was in *A La Broadway* in 1911. At 18 she was discovered by the *New York Times*, whose reviewer wrote a *"girl named Mae West, hitherto unknown, pleased by her grotesquerie and snappy way of singing and dancing."*[196] After roles in other shows, in 1926 she wrote, produced and starred in a play titled *Sex*, which was raided. She was sentenced to ten days, serving eight, for "corrupting the morals of youth." The incident enhanced her career and she went on to write more such plays resulting in packed houses. In 1932 she was contracted by Paramount Pictures, who starred her in numerous films. She was voted one of the greatest female stars of all time.

Olivia Wilde (March 10, 1984-_____) American actress, producer and model
Birth Name — Olivia Jane Cockburn

2010 Comic Con, San Diego, *Gage Skidmore*, Creative Commons Attribution- Share Alike

Olivia was born in New York City to a British journalist father, Andrew Cockburn, and American journalist mother, Leslie (Redlich) Cockburn, who was also a producer for CBS news magazine, 60 Minutes. Olivia is from an upper-class British family with an impressive pedigree. Aspiring to act since age two, she attended prestigious schools, studying acting at Gaiety School of Acting in Dublin. She chose the stage name Wilde after Irish author, Oscar Wilde.[197] After appearing in movies, she became known for her role on Fox's teen drama *The O.C.* as Alex Kelly, then in 2007, after another short-lived role, she joined the cast of Fox's medical drama, *House*, as an internist, where she spent five years. During that time and since, she has appeared in numerous films such as *Year One* (2009), *Tron: Legacy* (2010), *The Change-Up* (2011), *In Time* (2011), *People Like Us* (2012), and *Her* (2013), and has starred in the films *Cowboys & Aliens* (2011), *The Incredible Burt Wonderstone* (2013), *Drinking Buddies* (2013), *Rush* (2013), and *The Lazarus Effect* (2015).

Flip Wilson (December 8, 1933 – November 25, 1998) African American comedian and actor
Birth Name — Cleve Wilson, Jr.

1970 **Publicity Photo,** Public Domain

Wilson was one of 10 children born to a father who worked as a handyman, and a mother who abandoned the family when he was 7 years old. After bouncing around to varying foster homes, at 16 he lied about his age to join the U.S. Air Force. He always had a funny story to tell and was asked to tour military bases to cheer up the servicemen. Claiming that he was always "flipped out," Wilson's barracks mates gave him the nickname "Flip,"[198] and he started using it as a stage name. After being discharged from the military, Flip started work as a bellhop at San Francisco's Manor Plaza Hotel. He was hired by the hotel's nightclub to play a drunken patron between shows. His character gained popularity so he got work all over the state. Eventually his act became more sophisticated. During the 1960s he was hired by the Apollo Theater in Harlem and became a favorite guest on *The Tonight Show, Laugh In,* and the *Ed Sullivan Show.* He won a Grammy for his comedy album *The Devil Made Me Buy this Dress,* and he became a regular on *Laugh In.* That year *The Flip Wilson Show* debuted on NBC, winning a Golden Globe.

201

Stevie Wonder (May 13. 1950-_____) American musician, songwriter, record producer, and instrumentalist
Birth Name — Steveland Hardaway Judkins (later, Morris)

1973, Motown, Public Domain

Stevie was born in Saginaw, Michigan, six weeks premature, which, along with conditions in the hospital, resulted in retinopathy of prematurity, causing detachment of his retinas leading to blindness. At his age four, his mother left his father moving to Detroit with her children. She took back her maiden name of Morris and changed Stevie's name to Morris, partly because of relatives. Stevie began playing piano, harmonica and drums at an early age, forming a singing partnership, Stevie and John, with a friend. In 1961, at age 11, he sang an original song to **Ronnie White** of **The Miracles**, who took him to audition at Motown. When signing Stevie to Motown Records Tamla Label, **Clarence Paul** gave him the name **Little Stevie Wonder,**[199] and he truly was a wonder! A child prodigy, his blindness did anything but slow him down. He has recorded more than 30 top ten hits and won 25 Grammys, the most ever won by a solo artist. He was celebrated by *Billboard Magazine* as one of the "Hot 100 All-Time Pop Artists" in 2008.

Natalie Wood (July 20, 1938 – November 29, 1981) American film and television actress
Birth Name — Natalia Nikolaevna Zakharenko

1961, Warner Bros., Public Domain

Her parents had first emigrated from Russia to Quebec, then to San Francisco, California, where Natalie was born. In her youth her family told her mysterious tales about being gypsies or landowning aristocrats. Her mother told her that in her youth she had dreamed of becoming an actress, something that seemed to be transferred to her. Her mother took her to movies as a toddler and told her that the cameraman who pointed the camera lens at the audience at the end of the Paramount news reels was taking her picture. She believed her and smiled at the camera. After the family moved to Santa Rosa, during a film shoot, Natalie was noticed by the producers. The family had changed their surname to Gurdin, and moving to Los Angeles, her mother pursued an acting career for Natalie, often known as Natasha. After signing with RKO Pictures, **David Lewis** and **William Goetz** changed her name to Natalie Wood.[200] After parts as a child, then on television, Wood was best known for her screen roles in *Miracle on 34th Street*, *Splendor in the Grass*, *Rebel Without a Cause*, and *West Side Story*. She died mysteriously at sea.

Tiger Woods (December 20, 1975-_____) American pro golfer
Birth Name — Eldrick Tont Woods

2014, Bethesda, MD,
Keith Allison, Creative Commons Attribution- Share Alike

Born in Cypress, California, he is the only child of his parents' marriage. His father is African-American and his mother is from Thailand, and is mixed Thai, Chinese and Dutch. Woods' first name was coined from his parents' names and his middle name is a traditional Thai name. He was nicknamed Tiger in honor of his father's friend Col. Vuong Dang Phong, who had also been known as Tiger.[201]

Growing up in Orange County, California, Tiger was a child prodigy and was introduced to golf by his skilled father before the age of two. Before age three he putted against **Bob Hope** on the **Mike Douglas** Show. At three he shot 48 on nine holes on the Cypress Naval Course, and at five, he was in *Golf Digest* and on ABC's *That's Incredible*. As a teen he impressed the great **Jack Nicholas**. He is one of the most successful and highest paid golfers of all times, winning the 1997 Masters by 12 strokes. His career took a great hit in December 2009 amid allegations and later admissions of marital infidelity.

204

Ed Wynn (November 9, 1886 – June 19, 1966) American comedian/actor
Birth Name — Isaiah Edwin Leopold

1940s Publicity Photo, Public Domain

Born in Philadelphia, Pennsylvania, he was the son of a Jewish father from Bohemia and a mother of Romanian and Turkish ancestry from Istanbul. At 15, he quit school and soon ran away from home, working as a hat salesman and utility boy. He began in vaudeville in 1903, and stared in the **Ziegfeld Follies** starting in 1913. He adapted his middle name Edwin into his stage name, Ed Wynn, to save his family the embarrassment of having a lowly comedian as a relative.[202] In the next decades he wrote and directed numerous Broadway shows. His giggly wavering voice, by which he was known, was developed for the 1921 musical revue, *A Perfect Fool*. In the early 1930s he hosted a popular radio show, *The Fire Chief*, heard all across North America on Tuesday nights, sponsored by Texaco. His Fire Chief character was utilized in two movies: *Follow the Leader* (1930) and *The Chief* (1933). Wynn was offered the title role in the *Wizard of Oz* and turned it down. In 1949 and '50 he hosted one of the first comedy-variety TV shows, winning both a Peabody and an Emmy Award. After many films, he was the voice of various Disney characters.

Jay Z (December 4, 1969-_____) American rapper, record producer and entrepreneur
Birth Name — Shawn Corey Carter

2011, New York, Carter Foundation, Retouched, Creative Commons Attribution- Share Alike

Carter was born and raised by his mother in Brooklyn, New York after his father abandoned the family, where he attended one high school with future rapper, **AZ**, then another with fellow future rappers **The Notorious B.I.G.** and **Busta Rhymes**. He never graduated high school and according to rap lyrics was involved in selling drugs and was shot at three times. According to his mother he would wake up his siblings at night beating out drum patterns on the kitchen table until she bought him a boom box for his birthday, after which he began writing lyrics. He was known by the nickname Jazzy in his neighborhood, which led to his stage name of Jay-Z, changed to Jay Z on July 18, 2013. It also pays tribute to his musical mentor, **Jazz-O**,[203] on whose early recordings in the late '80s Jay Z can briefly be heard. With no major record deal, at first he sold CDs of his car, but in '96 he released his debut album, *Reasonable Doubt*, distributed by Priority. He is now one of the most successful hip-hop artists ever, winning 21 Grammys and selling 100 million + records.

NAME CHANGE REFERENCES

[1]Page 7: Winkler, Peter L. (October 30, 2009). "Nick Adams: His Hollywood Life and Death" crimemagazine.com.

[2]Page 8: Alda, Alan. *Never Have Your Dog Stuffed*, 2006, Random House New York, ISBN 0-8129-7440-9

[3]Page 9): *Encyclopedia Britannica* Online article: Woody Allen http://www.britannica.com/EBchecked/topic/16217/Woody-Allen

[4]Page 10: Spindle, Les. *Julie Andrews: A Bio-Bibliography*, Greenwood Press (1989)] ISBN 0-313-26223-3. pp. 1–2

[5]Page 11: Bio Marc Anthony. Online http://www.biography.com/people/marc-anthony-241193

[6]Page 12: *Desi Arnaz Facts*, Your Dictionary *Lucy and Desi*, par. 3 http://biography.yourdictionary.com/desi-arnaz

[7]Page 13: Marine Corp Records, Bernice Frankel; National Archives and Records Administration, Washington, DC

[8]Page 14: Bob Thomas, *The Man, The Dancer: The Life of Fred Astaire*, St. Martin's Press, New York, NY, 1987. ISBN 978-0312057831

[9] Page 15: Smithsonian.com : Black, Jonathan, Smithsonian Magazine August, 2009: *Charles Atlas: Muscle Man* http://www.smithsonianmag.com/ist/?next=/history/charles-atlas-muscle-man-34626921/?all

[10]Page 16: Fun Trivia: http://www.funtrivia.com/en/Celebrities/Autry-Gene-21301.html

[11]Page 17: Loren Bacall Profile http://www.filmreference.com/film/96/Lauren-Bacall.html

[12] Sperber, Ann M.; Lax, Eric (April 1997). *Bogart*. New York: Morrow. p. 246. ISBN 978-0688075392.

[13] Page 18: Conservapedia: the Trustworthy Encyclopedia, Article David Akeman http://www.conservapedia.com/David_Akeman

[14] Page 19: Bio.com *Pat Benatar* http://www.biography.com/people/pat-benatar-213028

[15] Page 20: COED.com *The 17 Known Girlfriends of Hugh Hefner (In Order of Hotness)*, April 14, 2010: http://coed.com/2010/04/14/the-17-known-girlfriends-of-hugh-hefner-in-order-of-hotness/

[16] Page 21: Assayas, Michka (2005). *Bono on Bono: Conversations with Michka Assayas*. London: Hodder & Stoughton. ISBN 0-340-83276-2.

[17] Page 22: Texas State Historical Association article: RICHARDSON, JILES PERRY (BIG BOPPER) htpp://tshaonline.org/handbook/online/articles/fri40

[18] Page 23: Lil' Bow Wow: Puppy Power (Page 2) MTV News. 2000-09-01

[19] Page 24: Madam Noire; http://madamenoire.com/ 448926/ celebrities-whose-real-names-you-never-knew/5/

[20] Page 25: Encyclopedia of World Biography: Charles Bronson http://www.notablebiographies.com/newsmakers2/2004-A-Di/Bronson-Charles.html

[21] Page 26: McCall, Cheryl. "Psst! Albert Brooks Isn't Kin to Mel Except in Comedy." *people.com*

[22] Page 27: Answers.com http://www.answers.com/Q/Why_did_Melvin_Kaminsky_change_his _name_to_Mel_Brooks

[23]Page 28: Hollywood Memoir.com *Red Buttons Comedian Dies at 87*
http://www.hollywoodmemoir.com/red-buttons

[24]Page 29: Biography.com *Nicolas Cage Biography*
http://www.biography.com/people/nicolas-cage-9234498

[25]Page 30: Biography.com *Michael Caine Biography*
http://www.biography.com/people/michael-caine-9234754

[26]Page 31: *10 Things You Might Not Have Known about Truman Capote*
http://mentalfloss.com/article/59198/10-things-you-might-not-have-known-about-truman-capote

[27]Page 32: Cohen, Morton (1996). *Lewis Carroll: A Biography*. Vintage Books. Pp100–104. ISBN 978-0-679-74562-4

[28]Page 33: "Cyd Charisse dies in LA at 86", yahoo.com, June 17, 2008

[29]Page 34: Charo
http://www.scottstander.com/Personalities/charo.html

[30]Page 35: Biography.com Chevy Chase Biography
http://www.biography.com/people/chevy-chase-9542517

[31]Page 36: Biography.com: Jessica Chastain
http://www.biography.com/people/jessica-chastain-20830013

[32]Page 37: [1] Arlene Brief Entertainment: Chubby Checker
http://arlenebriefentertainment.com/chubby-checker

[33]Page 38: http://ebook.worldlibrary.net/articles/Artist_name

[34]Page 39: Biography.com Patsy Cline
http://www.biography.com/people/patsy-cline-9251222

[35]Page 40: The Origins of Stage Names: Fabian Forte
http://rateyourmusic.com/list/ByteMe/the_origins_of_stage_names/

[36]Page 41: Steinberg, Jay: *Gary Cooper: The Pride of Hollywood*. 5-16-11
http://www.moviefanfare.com/gary-cooper-the-pride-of-hollywood/

[37]Page 42: Byron Fay: *Fayfare's Opry Blog*, 3-1-2015
http://fayfare.blogspot.com/2015/03/hawkshaw-hawkinscowboy-copas-final-opry.html

[38]Page 43: Encyclopedia Britannica: *David Copperfield, American Entertainer*
http://www.britannica.com/EBchecked/topic/711015/David-Copperfield

[39]Page 44: Elvis Costello, interview by Terry Gross, *Fresh Air from WHYY*, National Public Radio, WHYY-FM, Philadelphia, 28 February 1989 (rebroadcast 14 September 2007).

[40]Page 45: Newquist, Roy: *Conversations with Joan Crawford* (Citadel Press, New York, 1980) (Crawford, quoted in *Newquist*, pg. 31)

[41]Page 46: Answers.com Why did Tom Cruise Change His Name
http://www.answers.com/Q/Why_did_Tom_Cruise_change_his_name
Answered by "The Community"

[42]Page 47: France, Lisa Respers (August 25, 2009). "'Eraserhead' director inspired Billy Ray Cyrus". CNN.

[43]Page 48: Sutro, Dirk (April 20, 2011). *Jazz For Dummies*. John Wiley & Sons. p. 112. ISBN 978-1-118-06852-6.

[44]Page 49: Famous Name Changes
http://www.famousnamechanges.net/html/actor/actord.htm, and
http://www.sfgate.com/news/article/SANDRA-DEE-1942-2005-Actress-who-created-2728667.php

[45]Page 50: Bock, Paula, The Seattle Times, Seattle Washington, *Delilah, When Darkness Falls...*December 12, 1999

http://community.seattletimes.nwsource.com/archive/?date=19991212&slug=3000812

[46]Page 51: Harris, Paul, *The Guardian, Lana Del Rey: the Strange Story of the Star Who Re-wrote her Past,* New York, NY, 2014
http://www.theguardian.com/music/2012/jan/21/lana-del-rey-pop

[47]Page 52: "The New Christy Minstrels". Thenewchristyminstrels.com.
http://www.thenewchristyminstrels.com/

[48]Page 53: Name Candy: *Shakespeare Names, The Merchant of Venice* (blog) 2010. http://www.namecandy.com/celebrity-baby-names/blog/2010/07/20/shakespeare-names-the-merchant-of-venice
Kort, Michele (13 September 2005) *"Portia heart and soul"*. The Advocate.

[49]Page 54: Famous Name Changes
http://www.famousnamechanges.net/html/actor/actord.htm

[50]Page 55: New York Times, May 24, 1998: *John Derek, 71, Actor Known as Wife's Svengali, Is Dead*
http://www.nytimes.com/1998/05/24/nyregion/john-derek-71-actor-known-as-wife-s-svengali-is-dead.html

[51]Page 56: Sharon Osbourne interviews Dido (16 October 2003). *The Sharon Osbourne Show.*It's Dido Florian Cloud de Bounevialle O'Malley Armstrong when asked to say her real name.

[52]Page 57: Romero, Frances: *Time: Top 10 Most Ridiculous Celebrity Name Changes,* September 16, 2011
http://content.time.com/time/specials/packages/article/0,28804,2093588_2093587_2093580,00.html

[53]Page 58: Posner, Michael (2006-12-18). "A reluctant author of bestsellers". *Globe and Mail* (London).

[54]Page 59: del Castillo, Michael, *What's in a name change, Snoop Dogg? Lessons on rebranding yourself* , October 21, 2013 http://upstart.bizjournals.com/entrepreneurs/hot-shots/2013/10/21/snoop-dogg-changes-name-to-snoopzilla.html?page=all

[55]Page 60: Douglas, Kirk (2007). *Let's face it: 90 years of living, loving, and learning.* John Wiley and Sons. P. 3. ISBN 0-470-08469-3.

[56]Page 61: TV Personality/Singer Mike Douglas Dies at 81 http://www.billboard.com/articles/news/57559/tv-personalitysinger-mike-douglas-dies-at-81

[57]Page 62: Trackk: *Bob Dylan: Zimmy, Bobby, Zimbo, Blind Boy Grunt, The Voice of Protest, The Voice of a Generation* https://tackk.com/n41v6d [2] Shelton, Robert, *No Direction Home: The Life and Music of Bob Dylan.* Originally published 1966, De Capo Press, NY 2003

[58]Page 63: Hughes, Annika M: *Mary Ann Evans and George Eliot: One Woman* http://www.womeninworldhistory.com/imow-Eliot.pdf

[59]Page 64: Electra, Carmen: https://www.youtube.com/watch?v=phdrqZBJsyI

[60]Page 65: Dale Evans Biography http://www.royrogers.com/dale_evans_bio.html

[61]Page 66: Famous Birthdays: Linda Evans, TV Actress http://www.famousbirthdays.com/people/linda-evans.html

[62]Page 67: http://www.morganfairchildtribute.com/profile.html

[63]Page 68: Thomas, Robert McG., Jr. The New York Times, Jan. 9, 1996: Minnesota Fats, a Real Hustler With a Pool Cue, Is Dead

http://www.nytimes.com/1996/01/19/sports/minnesota-fats-a-real-hustler-with-a-pool-cue-is-dead.html

[64]Page 69: Oridean, Toby, *Black Eyed Pea's Singer Fergie Officially Changes Her Name* August 17, 1913
http://archive.entertainmentwise.com/news/123861/Black-Eyed-Peas-Singer-Fergie-Officially-Changes-Her-Name

[65]Page 70: The Famous People: Flavor Flav Biography
http://www.thefamouspeople.com/profiles/flavor-flav-4001.php

[66]Page 71: "Gerald R. Ford Genealogical Information". *Gerald R. Ford Presidential Library & Museum*. University of Texas.

[67]Page 72: http://www.lifetimetv.co.uk/biography/biography-jodie-foster

[68]Page 73: Michael J. Fox Fast Facts, CNN
http://www.cnn.com/2013/05/24/us/michael-j-fox-fast-facts/

[69]Page 74: Jamie Foxx Net Worth: About Jamie Foxx
http://getnetworth.net/jamie-foxx-net-worth/

[70]Page 75: Redd Fox Biography
http://www.biography.com/people/redd-foxx-9300106

[71]Page 76: IMBd Anthony Franciosa Biography
http://www.imdb.com/name/nm0290047/bio

[72]Page 77: Dictionary.com Blog: Is she a "lady"? Is she "gaga"? Did Lady Gaga choose her name because of what it literally means?
http://blog.dictionary.com/lady-gaga/

[73]Page 78: Garbo Forever: The Legend Lives On
http://www.garboforever.com/Garbos_Lovers-Friends-07.htm

[74]Page 79: Judy Garland: A Brief Biography
http://judygarland.com/id1.html

[75]Page 80: Elma Napier http://en.kwizy.org/wiki/Elma_Napier

[76]Page 81: James Garner Interview at Archive of American Television;
Google Video, March 17, 1999

[77]Page 82: Tracey Gold Biography
http://www.biography.com/people/tracey-gold-585036

[78]Page 83: Berry, Allison, Time Magazine, Carlyn Johnson to Whoopi
Goldberg, Sept. 16, 2011
http://content.time.com/time/specials/packages/article/0,28804,20935
88_2093587_2093597,00.html

[79]Page 84: Frequently Asked Questions
http://www.carygrant.net/faq.html#citizen

[80]Page 85: The Telegraph, Macy Gray Interview: 'I was a clown'
http://www.telegraph.co.uk/culture/7741360/Macy-Gray-interview-I-
was-a-clown.html

[81]Page 86: Bennett, Linda Greene (November 1, 2004). *My Father's
Voice: The Biography of Lorne Greene* (Paperback ed.). iUniverse, Inc.
p. 254. ISBN 978-0-595-33283-0.

[82]Page 87: Ann Harding: A Q&A With Biographer Scott O'Brien
http://moviemorlocks.com/2010/12/08/ann-harding-a-q-a-with-
biographer-scott-obrien/

[83]Page 88: Discography of Hawkshaw Hawkins, Biography
http://hawkshaw-hawkins.musikear.com/

[84]Page 89: Spoto, Donald (2006). "Chapter One: 1929–1939". *Enchantment: The Life of Audrey Hepburn*. New York, NY: Harmony Books. ISBN 0-307-23758-3. OCLC 779029693

[85]Page 90: "'O. Henry' on Himself, Life, and Other Things" (PDF), *New York Times*, April 4, 1909, p. SM9

[86] Page 91: Raymond, Emile (2006), *From My Cold, Dead Hands: Charlton Heston and American Politics*, University of Kentucky Press, p. 321, ISBN 0813171490

[87]Page 92: Hulk Hogan (2009). *My Life Outside the Ring*. St. Martin's Press, New York, NY p. 77 ISBN 9780312588892.

[88]Page 93: Rock and Roll Hall of Fame: Billie Holiday Biography https://rockhall.com/inductees/billie-holiday/bio/

[89]Page 94: McDonald, Les (2010), *The Day the Music Died*. Xlibris Corp. ISBN 978-1-469-11356-2, p. 17

[90]Page 95: Quirk, Lawrence J. (1998). *Bob Hope: The Road Well-Traveled*. New York: Applause. ISBN 978-1-55783-353-2.

[91]Page 96: New World Encyclopedia, *Harry Houdini* http://www.newworldencyclopedia.org/entry/Harry_Houdini

[92]Page 97: Berger, Joseph, "Rock Hudson, Screen Idol Dies at 59," *The New York Times*," October 3, 1985.

[93]Page 98: *The Telegraph*, London UK, *Eurovision 2012: How Engelbert Humperdinck really got his name*, Saturday April 4, 2015

[94]Page 99: The Daily Sparkle, April 2015 http://static1.1.sqspcdn.com/static/f/456574/26068546/1427117762090/April+Fas+facts+proofed+2015.pdf?token=zSrFxcuEb0gJOAg3WSKMztrZQy4%3D

[95]Page 100: How Ice Cube Got His Name: On the Record
https://www.youtube.com/watch?v=otQUAqmLOjY

[96]Page 101: Zackarin, Jordan, Huffington Post, *Vanilla Ice On Real Estate, DIY Show And How He Got That Name*, 6-2-2011
http://www.huffingtonpost.com/2011/06/02/vanilla-ice-talks-diy-show-name_n_870170.html

[97]Page 102: Century, Ice-T and Douglas, *Ice: A Memoir of Gangster Life and Redemption-- from South Central to Hollywood*, p. 41; One World Books (Random House), 2011, ISBN 978-0-345-52328-7

[98]Page 103: Edmonds, Ben, untitled essay in Greatest Hits, 2001

[99]Page 104: David Janssen, Find A Grave
http://www.findagrave.com/cgi-bin/fg.cgi?page=gr&GRid=1672

[100]Page 105: Elton John Biography
http://www.notablebiographies.com/Ho-Jo/John-Elton.html

[101]Page 106: CMT Artists: About Grandpa Jones
http://www.cmt.com/artists/grandpa-jones-00/biography/

[102]Page 107: Jennifer Jones Biography, IMDb
http://www.imdb.com/name/nm0428354/bio

[103]Page 108[1]: Huey, Steve: The Judds' Biography
http://www.allmusic.com/artist/the-judds-mn0000086312/biography

[104]Wynonna Judd, Encyclopedia.com
http://www.encyclopedia.com/topic/Wynonna_Judd.aspx

[105]Page 109: Diane Keaton Biography, IMDb
http://www.imdb.com/name/nm0000473/bio

[106]Page 110: Keaton, Eleanor; Vance, Jeffrey (2001). *Buster Keaton Remembered.* Harry N. Abrams Inc. p. 124. ISBN 9780810942271

[107]Page 111: Vineyard, Chloe (January 18, 2006). *Alicia Keys Nearly Spills Secrets To Jane. MTV News.*

[108]Page 112: Christina and Jordana (July 5, 2010). *Goodbye Larry King.* Schema Magazine.

[109]Page 113: *Ben Kingsley Tells Letterman Why He Changed His Name* https://lakshmigandhi.wordpress.com/2010/02/18/ben-kingsley-tells-letterman-why-he-changed-his-name/

[110]Page 114: Holt, Patricia (Patti LaBelle) http://pabook.libraries.psu.edu/palitmap/bios/Labelle_Patti.html

[111]Page 115: Weil, Martin (July 2, 1991*). TV Actor Michael Landon Dies; Star of Bonanza, Little House. Washington Post.* p. B04.

[112]Page 116: Ralph Lauren Biography http://www.biography.com/people/ralph-lauren-9374814

[113]Page 117: TV.com Joey Lawrence http://www.tv.com/people/joey-lawrence/

[114]Page 118: Booms Beat, 50 Interesting Fasts about John Legend http://www.boomsbeat.com/articles/7411/20140805/50-interesting-facts-about-john-legend-he-was-his-high-schools-prom-king-he-majored-in-english.htm

[115]Page 119: IMDb Biography: Tea Leoni http://www.imdb.com/name/nm0000495/bio

[116]Page 120: Bio.com: Sophia Loren http://www.biography.com/people/sophia-loren-9386318

[117]Page 121: School Project for Technology: Joe Louis' Amateur Career
http://brownbomber.weebly.com/joe-louis-amateur-career.html

[118]Page 122: Behind the Name
http://www.behindthename.com/name/courtney/comments
Sounes, Howard A History of the 27 Club Through the Lives of Brian
Jones, Jimi Hendrix ...
https://books.google.com/books?id=NWT9CAAAQBAJ&pg=PA104&I
pg=PA104&dq=courtney+love+stage+name&source=bl&ots=rJVB8VAQ
uq&sig=WJ0SZGYn4JBsfNvceNt7hBhUQy4&hl=en&sa=X&ei=5WuJVdu
3Hov7gwTp0IHQDg&ved=0CHIQ6AEwDw#v=onepage&q=courtney%
20love%20stage%20name&f=false
http://www.imdb.com/name/nm0001482/bio

[119]Page 123 : Kotsilibas-Davis, James; Loy, Myrna (1987). *Myrna Loy: Being and Becoming.* Alfred A. Knopf ISBN 0-394-55593-7, pp 42-43

[120]Page 124: Daily Writing Tips, Ludicrous Vs Ridiculous
http://www.dailywritingtips.com/ludicrous-vs-ridiculous/

[121]Page 125: *Above* Magazine (Fall 2008). "Body Talk with Elle Macpherson", pp. 16–31

[122]Page 126: IMDb Lee Majors Biography
http://www.imdb.com/name/nm0000516/bio

[123]Page 127: Megan Smolenyak: Happy St. Patrick's Day, Barry Manilow! The Huffington Post. March 17, 2010

[124]Page 128: Hartmann, Graham, Loudwire: Marilyn Manson- Stage Name Origins: http://loudwire.com/marilyn-manson-stage-name-origins/

[125]Page 129: Lewis, Pete, *Bruno Mars: Out of this World!* Blues & Soul, Blues & Soul LCC; http://parade.com/125331/parade/how-bruno-mars-came-up-with-his-stage-name/

[126]Page 130: Grudens, Richard, *The Italian Crooners Bedside Companion*, page 120, 2005, Celebrity Files Publishing Co., Sunnybrook, NY, USA, ISBN 0-9763877-0-0

[127]Page 131: Encyclopedia.com Ricky Martin
http://www.encyclopedia.com/topic/Ricky_Martin.aspx

[128]Page 132: Nine People Who've Changed Their Names for Their Careers http://www.rifemagazine.co.uk/2015/06/nine-people-whove-changed-their-names-for-their-careers/

[129]Page 133: Sychak, Bret Michael (Bret Michaels)
http://pabook.libraries.psu.edu/palitmap/bios/Michaels__Bret.html

[130]Page 134: Where did Nicki Minaj get her name from?
http://nickiminajegoson.blogspot.com/2013/04/where-did-nicki-minaj-get-her-name-from.html

[131]Page 135: Biography.com Helen Mirren
http://www.biography.com/people/helen-mirren-547434

[132]Page 136: Where did the name Marilyn Monroe come from?
http://www.marilynmonroepages.com/name/

[133]Page 137: Moore, Clayton; Thompson, Frank: *I Was That Masked Man*, 1998, page 50, Taylor Trade Publishing, 978-0878332168 and
Eiss, Harry Shadows in the Fog, page 146
https://books.google.com/books?id=IxwrBwAAQBAJ&pg=PA146&dq=the+name+Clayton+Moore&hl=en&sa=X&ei=5XONVcLECoavggTBiKGIBQ&ved=0CEgQ6AEwBA#v=onepage&q=the%20name%20Clayton%20Moore&f=false

[134]Page 138: Stage Name vs. Birth Name: Demi Moore's Real Name
http://www.namecandy.com/celebrity-baby-names/blog/2009/10/20/stage-name-vs-birth-name-demi-moores-real-name

[135]Page 139: Back of the Cereal Box: Too Many Dinty Moores
http://www.backofthecerealbox.com/2008/02/too-many-dinty-moores.html

[136]Page 140: Encyclopedia Britannica
http://www.britannica.com/biography/Julianne-Moore

[137]Page 141: "Grandma Moses in the 21st Century (originally published in *Resource Library Magazine.*)". Traditional Fine Arts Organization Inc.

[138]Page 142: Answers at Yahoo
https://answers.yahoo.com/question/index?qid=20130625195730AAk6nwG

[139]Page 143: Max Lief, Buffalo Sunday Express, July 20, 1924, *The Real Inside Dope on the Movie Stars: Naldi Leads in Rise of Nonna Dooley — Looks Before Brains Says Film Vamp.* http://nitanaldi.com/wp-content/uploads/2010/11/Buffalo_Sunday_Express_7-20-1924.pdf

[140]Page 144: Annie Oakley Foundation
http://www.annieoakleyfoundation.org/newsletters/no14.pdf

[141]Page 145: Taylor, DJ: *Orwell: The Life* (2003), page 126. Henry Holt and Company, London, England. ISBN 978-0805074734
https://answers.yahoo.com/question/index?qid=20070211040134AAV348T

[142]Page 146: *About Buck*, Rich McKienzle the biography at Owens'official website adapted from Kienzle's notes for **Rhino Records'** 1992 "The Buck Owens Collection" box set
http://www.newworldencyclopedia.org/entry/Buck_Owens

[143]Page 147: Minnie Pearl Inductee Biography, Country Music Hall of Fame

website. http://countrymusichalloffame.org/Inducteesview/minnie-pearl

[144]Page 148: Cutforth, Dan, Lipsitz, Jane (directors); Perry, Katy (autobiographer) July 5, 2012. *Katy Perry: Part of Me* (Motion picture). United States; Imagine Entertainment. Perry Productions et al, Paramount Pictures

[145]Page 149: Speace, Geri. "Bernadette Peters Biography". MusicianGuide.com, Encyclopedia.com, Bernadette Peters http://www.encyclopedia.com/topic/Bernadette_Peters.aspx

[146]Page 150: Pro Rodeo Hall of Fame: Slim Pickens http://www.prorodeohalloffame.com/inductees/by-category/contract-personnel/slim-pickens/

[147]Page 151: Biography.com: Pink http://www.biography.com/people/pink-562098

[148]Page 152: KSFM1045 http://ksfm.cbslocal.com/photo-galleries/2011/12/19/20-things-you-didnt-know-about-pitbull/axe-lounge-late-night-at-super-bowl-2/

[149]Page 153: Lilton, Sarah, Natalie Portman: A Biography http://www.hyperink.com/Natalie-Portman-A-Biography-b1685

[150]Page 154: *Why did William James Adams Black Eyed Peas change his name to Will.i.am?* http://www.answers.com/Q/Why_did_William_James_Adams_Black_Eyed_Peas_change_his_name_to_Will.i.am

[151]Page 155: Mariani, John F., *How Italian Food Conquered the World*, Page 165, Palgrave MacMillan, New York, NY, 2011, ISBN 908-0-230-10439-6

[152]Page 156: Della Reese Biography
http://www.imdb.com/name/nm0005343/bio

[153]Page 157: Superman Homepage
http://www.supermanhomepage.com/tv/tv.php?topic=cast-crew/george-reeves

[154]Page 158: Anne Rice Biography, AnneRice.com

[155]Page 159: History is Queer
http://historyisqueer.tumblr.com/post/43833021171/history-is-queer-little-richard

[156]Page 160: Robbins, Jann: Harold and Me: My Life, Love, and Hard Times with Harold Robbins, Macmillan, New York, NY, 2009 ISBN 978-0-7653-0003-4

[157]Page 161: IMDb Biography: Ginger Rogers
http://www.imdb.com/name/nm0001677/bio

[158]Page 162: Encyclopedia.com Roy Rogers
http://www.encyclopedia.com/topic/Roy_Rogers.aspx

[159]Page 163: Biography.com: Mickey Rooney
http://www.biography.com/people/mickey-rooney-9463300

[160]Page 164: Parish, James Robert, *The Hollywood Book of Breakups* 2006 John Wiley & Sons, Hoboken, NJ ISBN 978-0-471-75268-4

[161]Page 165: Wills, Dominic, Winona Ryder Biography
http://www.talktalk.co.uk/entertainment/film/biography/artist/winona-ryder/biography/135

[162]Page 166: Quarterman, John, *Isla St. Clair – A Little More Background*
http://sinclair.quarterman.org/archive/2000/11/msg00557.html

[163]Page 167: Fensch, Thomas (2001). *The Man Who Was Dr. Seuss*. Woodlands: New Century Books. p. 38. ISBN 0-930751-11-6. ; Cohen, Charles (2004). *The Seuss, the Whole Seuss and Nothing But the Seuss: A Visual Biography of Theodor Seuss Geisel*. Random House Books for Young Readers. p. 86. ISBN 0-375-82248-8. OCLC 53075980

[164]Page 168 Nightingale, Benedict (16 October 1988). "Jane Seymour, Queen of the Mini-Series." *The New York Times*

[165]Page 169, 170 Ramirez, Erika (February 28, 2011). "The True Identity of Charlie Sheen: Tracing the Roots of The Estevez Family". Latina magazine

[166]Page 169, 170: Fun Trivia
http://www.funtrivia.com/askft/Question120477.html

[167]Page 171: Kirsch, Jonathan, Los Angeles Times (2 February 2007) *Sheldon's Writing Spoke to the Masses*
http://articles.latimes.com/2007/feb/02/entertainment/et-sheldon2

[168]Page 172: Paul Brock's Music Liner Notes: Dinah Shore
https://musiclinernotes.wordpress.com/page/14/

[169]Page 173: Jewish Virtual Library: Gene Simmons
https://www.jewishvirtuallibrary.org/jsource/biography/Gene_Simmons.html

[170]Page 174: Graham, John, Occidental Observer (May 26, 2011) Mrs. Dominique Strauss-Kahn: Female Version Worse
http://www.theoccidentalobserver.net/2011/05/mrs-dominique-strauss-kahn-female-version-worse/

[171]Page 175: Biography.com Nikki Sixx
http://www.biography.com/people/nikki-sixx-20854163#synopsis

[172]Page 176: Perper, Joshua A., MD; Cina, Stephen J., MD. (22 June 2010) *When Doctors Kill, Who, Why and How,* p. 214. Copernicus Books, New York, NY. ISBN 978-1-4419-1368-5

[173]Page 177: IMDb. Suzanne Somers Biography
http://www.imdb.com/name/nm0001755/bio

[174]Page 178: Frank Souter, uncle to Joe South (1968), Atlanta, Georgia, personal friend of Stanley J. St. Clair, author

[175]Page 179: Biography.com: Dusty Springfield
http://www.biography.com/people/dusty-springfield-9491157#early-years

[176]Page 180: Rawlings, Nate (September 16, 2011) Time Steven Demetre Georgiou to Cat Stevens to Yusuf Islam

[177]Salon: http://www.salon.com/1999/08/14/cat_2/

[178]Page 181: The Smoking Gun Archive: Names in the News (June 20, 2001) http://www.thesmokinggun.com/documents/celebrity/names-news

[179]Page 182: The Eagle Eye. The Vault: Disco Diva Donna Summer
https://lhueagleeye.wordpress.com/2015/04/19/the-vault-disco-diva-donna-summer/

[180]Page 183: Minny's Musings – Women of Courage
http://patsblogminnysmusings.com/tag/mother-teresa/

[181]Page 184: Celeb R.E. Hip Hop Star Akon Settles Down in Woodland Hills http://sanfernandovalleyblog.blogspot.com/2014/04/celeb-re-hip-hop-star-akon-settles-down.html

[182]Page 185: Cohn, Art (November 9, 1958). "The Nine Lives of Michael Todd: A Hustler, He Never Looked Back". *The Miami News.* p. 1.

[183]Page 186: IMDb Biography, Rip Torn
http://www.imdb.com/name/nm0001800/bio

[184]Page 187: *The Aloha Cowboy*. *People*. **42** (9):36. September 14, 1994

[185]Page 188: Gulla, Bob (2008) *Icons of R&B and Soul: Ray Charles; Little Richard; Fats Domino; Ruth Brown; LaVern Baker; Sam Cooke; Jackie Wilson ; Etta James; Ike and Tina Turner; The Isley Brothers; James Brown*. p. 176. Greenwood Press, Westport, Connecticut. ISBN 978-0-313340-45-1

[186]Page 189:BoatSafe.com. What do Mark Twain and your depth sounder have in common?
http://www.boatsafe.com/nauticalknowhow/marktwain.htm

[187]Page 190: IMDb Biography, Shania Twain
http://www.imdb.com/name/nm0005510/bio

[188]Page 191: http://1155108050056.blogspot.com/2014/02/conway-twitty.html

[189]Page 192: Rudolph Valentino
http://cbrowder.blogspot.com/2014_06_01_archive.html

[190]Page 193: Official Facebook page of Jean Valli
https://www.facebook.com/pages/Jean-Valli/208356732184

[191]Page 194: Google Groups: Pauline Phillips, "Dear Abby" Abigail Van Buren, Dies at 94
https://groups.google.com/forum/#!topic/radical_faerie_activists/1235Bk2vmzg

[192]Page 195: **Bream, John:** Bobby Vee, Minnesota's first rock star, has Alzheimer's. http://www.startribune.com/bobby-vee-minnesota-s-first-rock-star-has-alzheimer-s/149735175/

[193]Page 196:   Roberts, Randy; Olson, James S. (1995). *John Wayne: American*. New York: Free Press. ISBN 978-0-02-923837-0.

[194]Page 197: Geni.com Tuesday Weld
http://www.geni.com/people/Tuesday-Weld/6000000004140759837

[195]Page 198: Biography.com. Dottie West
http://www.biography.com/people/dottie-west-196956#early-career

[196]Page 199: Voss, Joan, Sr. Connection
http://www.seniorconnectionnewspaper.com/features/2015/May/holl
ywood.php

[197]Page 200: Olivia Wilde's Real Name is Olivia Cockburn
http://www.omgfacts.com/lists/7802/Olivia-Wilde-s-real-name-is-
Olivia-Cockburn-ab735-6

[198]Page 201: Askville by Amazon- http://askville.amazon.com/drag-
character-Flip-Wilson/AnswerViewer.do?requestId=56964757

[199]Page 202: Stevie Wonder: Blind Faith, The Independent
http://www.independent.co.uk/news/people/profiles/stevie-wonder-
blind-faith-865838.html

[200]Page 203: Lambert, Gavin (2004). *Natalie Wood: A Life* (Biography). P. 30
London: Faber and Faber. ISBN 978-0-571-22197-4

[201]Page 204: Callahan, Tom (May 9, 2006). "Tiger's dad gave us all some
lessons to remember". *Golf Digest*

[202]Page 205: Ed Wynn Show 2. http://itube247.com/ed-wynn-show-2/

[203]Page 206: Birchmeier, Jason. Jay-Z Biography. Allmusic.

ENTRANTS WITH DIRECT OR INDIRECT PERSONAL, FAMILY, FRIEND OR BUSINESS CONNECTIONS TO THE AUTHOR

www.ingramcontent.com/pod-product-compliance
Lightning Source LLC
Chambersburg PA
CBHW051954090426
42741CB00008B/1392